For my lovely mum,
a truly excellent human.

Kitchen KEEPERS

Real-Life Recipes to Make on Repeat

KATRINA MEYNINK

Hardie Grant

BOOKS

MAKING FRIENDS with SALAD

MY NAME IS KATRINA and I LIKE MINCE

BIG BOWLS of COMFORT

SOS SAVIOURS

EATING-OUT-LOUD LIP-SMACKERS

SIDESHOW ALLEY

GOOD THINGS for WEEKENDS

→

BAKING BENDERS

SMACK SNACKS

A few EASY DESSERTS

bonus recipe!

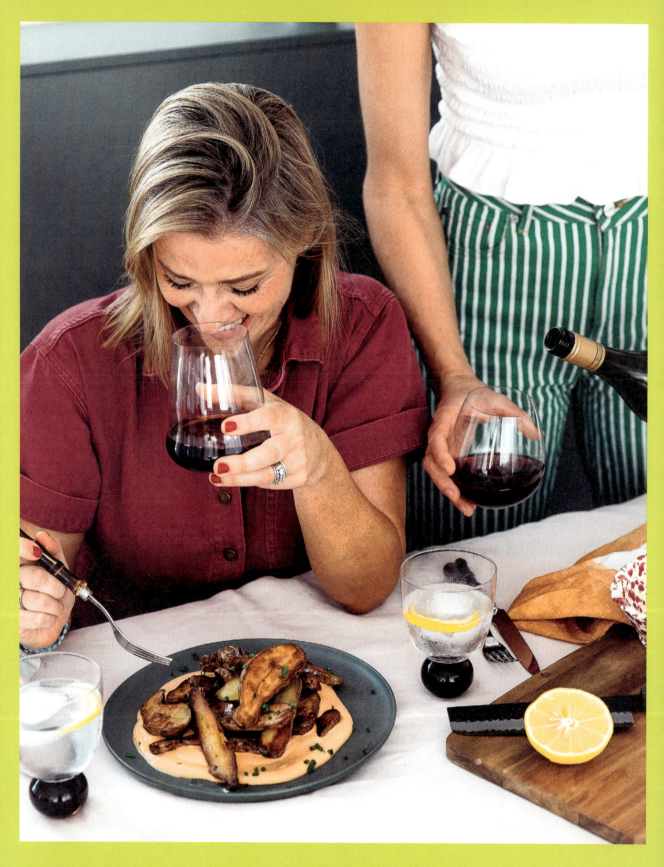

Friends, gather in. It's dinnertime again.

'What can we eat?' has got to be the most muttered phrase across households daily. Even when we absolutely love to cook, at times it can feel like a chore. Working out what, when and with which vegetable to prevent scurvy really does sometimes feel like it might be the straw that breaks the camel's back. I get it. I truly do.

I want this book to be useful, not idealistic. To give you a few ideas for Thursday night, for the slow-cook Sunday or the manic Monday. We're not rolling out fresh pasta midweek (how delightful would that be) or pulling a hot loaf of bread from the oven. We are, simply, doing our best. These are the meals I snatch out between squad sessions, a work deadline, a touch footy game, water polo training or a hip-hop class. Meals drawn from staring into the fridge at another bag of mince or that tin of tomatoes sitting solo in the pantry and wondering, where to from here?

In my family, the rhythm of life is in many ways marked by the meal in front of us. When we can fit it in, we have slow-cook Sundays; when the wheels are off and we need to hunker down, there will always be pasta. Dinner is a constant experiment in wabi-sabi – a daily squeeze of transience and imperfection. Our meals are equal parts sustenance and pleasure and, at times, they are the emotional bandaid we all need. If only there was more time.

And I know I am not alone, so this book is full of kitchen keepers: an offering of clear and uncomplicated recipes that are big on flavour while relatively low on effort. These recipes really do come from a starting point that toast is good any time of day – at a table, on the couch, in a bath (I'm dreaming) or in bed.

The recipes celebrate and curtail culinary largesse in equal measure. They are a combination of pantry staples, a few fumbles towards satisfying a craving and some recipes that luxuriate in those moments we still find to potter joyously at the stove.

There are special-occasion dishes for the times when you feel like setting the table, opening a bottle of wine, maybe even having a few friends around.

But there are also plenty of meals for the couch. Sometimes it's the best spot. Why else would everyone end up on it when the party's over?

And from one messy ~~life~~ kitchen to another, I hope you find yourself making these recipes on repeat and, most importantly, enjoying them with the people that you love. Because they are the very reason we are in the kitchen anyway.

Happy cooking!

BEFORE you GET STARTED

While I love to wax lyrical, I do acknowledge most cookbook authors could confess to murder in their recipe intros and their crimes could remain undiscovered for eternity, because absolutely no one reads them.

I feel the same way about the Magna Carta of lead-in pages detailing equipment, ingredients and pantry requirements, all the bits and bobs and the kitchen sink. Let's just get to the good stuff! So here are my flavour hacks, my secret serums for busy cooking. I can't live without them, and you'll always find them floating in my pantry or fridge to pull together dinner with a shortcut to flavour town.

FROM THE CUPBOARD

Sweet soy sauce

Soy sauce

Oyster sauce

Ground cumin

Ground coriander

Ground turmeric

Smoked almonds

Tomato paste (concentrated purée)

Yuzu kosho

Yeast flakes

Turkish red pepper flakes

French shallots, onions

Jarred roasted capsicums (bell peppers)

Liquid kombu/dashi

Milk powder

Crunchy chilli oil

Golden raisins

Honey mustard

All the pasta, all the beans, all the tinned fish

FROM THE FRIDGE

Sweet and spicy pickles (plus the juice)

Smoked semi-dried tomatoes

Cream

Parmesan

Feta

Capers

Buttermilk

FRESH STORES

Lemons

Garlic

Makrut lime leaves

Lemongrass

Absolutely anything and everything smoked!
Smoking creates instant caramelised flavour.
Add something smoked (seriously, anything)
and it will bring a depth of flavour in very little
time to every dish you make. You won't look back.

A NOTE ON OVENS

Oven temperatures in this book are for
conventional ovens. If using a fan-forced oven,
reduce the temperature by 20°C (35°F).

Weekend makes
for weekday breaks

Weekend makes will give you weekday
breaks. This is a handy reference list
of recipes that you could prepare at
least 80 per cent of in advance so
a midweek marvel can be pulled
together in a flash.

BOUGHT IT FOR this, BUT YOU CAN USE IT for THAT

How annoying are specialist ingredients or small-timeframe use-by dates?
Below are some ingredients that you might buy for a recipe in this book
and where you can use them up in others. Waste is not our friend.

INGREDIENT	RECIPE
Lemongrass	Turmeric lemongrass cold noodle salad **36**; Satay chicken pop tarts **60**; Spicy sichuan tomato shallot butter noodles **108**; Pork burgers with red curry and coriander mayo **158**; Fish curry, heavy on the lemongrass **112**
Golden raisins	Charred broccolini with brown butter mayo, party crunch and a few golden raisins **134**; A pimpin picadillo **48**
Roasted capsicum	Lamb meatballs with five-second romesco and herby fennel slaw **52**; White bean and couscous salad with roasted red pepper dressing **38**
Olives	Lamb meatballs with five-second romesco and herby fennel slaw **52**; A pimpin picadillo **48**; Lazy eggplant pasta with olives **64**; Saucy baked eggs **97**; Tuna pasta **82**
Sichuan pepper	Lemon and honey chicken **74**; Spicy sichuan tomato shallot butter noodles **108**
Cream	Wednesday night chicken saag **66**; Butter dal **70**; Turkish delight pav **224**; Blood plum pannacotta for a crowd with orange blossom and black pepper **222**; Lulu's honey mustard chicken drumsticks **81**
Buttermilk	Black bean and avo salad with curry and coriander buttermilk dressing **40**; Fruits of the forest and white chocolate muffins **194**; A very, very dependable chocolate cake **184**
Sour cream	Real deal sour cream and onion dip with non-negotiable Chicken Crimpies **198**; A very, very dependable chocolate cake **184**
Sobrasada	Pumpkin and sobrasada salad with hot honey feta dressing **32**; Chorizo, pumpkin and kale lasagne **156**
Crunchy chilli oil	Sweet potato 'n' greens spoon salad with crunchy chilli oil dressing **16**; Spicy watermelon and chunky cukes salad **34**; Peanut butter noodles **86**

Semi-dried tomatoes	Lazy eggplant pasta with olives **64**; Saucy baked eggs **97**; Pizza and four great toppings **152**
Mozzarella	Pizza and four great toppings **152**; Chorizo, pumpkin and kale lasagne **156**; Peach, buffalo moz and jalapeño salad with mint chimichurri **18**; Fried caper and roast capsicum panzanella **24**
Capers	Fried caper and roast capsicum panzanella **24**; Roasted fennel with Café de Paris sauce **170**; Saucy baked eggs **97**; Slow-cooked puttanesca onions **128**
Nutritional yeast flakes	Spicy sichuan tomato shallot butter noodles **108**; The crispiest of crispy prawn tacos with (not) drunk mayo **174**; Cabbage and kale slaw with chilli, yeast and seed dressing **20**

Recipe tags

It's ok I get it, you want to work smarter not harder. You might also like instant gratification where you can get it. I see you. Here are some handy reference symbols so you can instantly see how a recipe is going to work for you in your busy life.

 Freezes well

 Pantry winner

 Travels well

 Couch-friendly

 Hands-off cooking

 Multitasker

MAKING FRIENDS
with SALAD

I have an intense love of salads. A Romeo and Juliet kind of longing, equivalent to fervent missives on secret notes. You know, the kind of love reserved for the ages, history books and Sonny and Cher.

A salad improves any meal. It can be the meal, or it can happily share the limelight. Salads know how to share and play well with others.

I can't remember a day I've gone without salad of some form, so the fact this chapter isn't occupying half this book is a sign of my capacity for restraint and the long game.

These are real, in-your-face salads. No salads of lonely green leaves looking for friends but meal salads with oomph and texture and fill-you-up kind of sentiments. The salads that make you feel alive and the very best version of yourself, because it is, after all, salad.

Holy moly, this is delicious

SWEET POTATO 'N' GREENS SPOON SALAD with CRUNCHY CHILLI OIL DRESSING

If a salad had a 'cannot stop eating it' criteria, this one deserves first place. It slaps you in the face with its freshness and the nose-tingling zing chaser of chilli oil. The crunch of fresh peas is a must, but only when they are cheap and in season. Otherwise, you could replace them with edamame. Frozen peas won't work because you want the resistant crunch in play for the mouth-loving textural wonderland that is this salad.

1 kg (2 lb 3 oz) sweet potato, peeled and cut into roughly 1 cm (½ in) cubes

2 tablespoons olive oil

2 tablespoons soy sauce

2 tablespoons maple syrup

2 avocados, stone removed and cut into roughly 1 cm (½ in) cubes

3–4 Lebanese (short) cucumbers, cut into 1 cm (½ in) cubes

1 cup freshly podded peas (or edamame)

3 spring onions (scallions), finely sliced

leaves of 1 large bunch coriander (cilantro), finely chopped

DRESSING

3 tablespoons crunchy chilli oil

60 ml (2 fl oz/¼ cup) rice vinegar

1 tablespoon mirin

3 tablespoons maple syrup

2 tablespoons soy sauce

1 garlic clove, grated

2½ tablespoons freshly grated ginger

**SERVES 6–8
AS PART OF A SPREAD**

Preheat the oven to 170°C (340°F).

Spread the diced sweet potato in a single layer over a large, lined baking tray. Add the olive oil, soy sauce and maple syrup, and give everything a good mix around with your hands so that the sweet potato is well coated. Roast for 30 minutes, stirring well about halfway through to prevent burning. You want the sweet potato to be caramelised, golden on the edges and cooked through. Allow to cool on the tray.

Make the salad dressing by combining all the ingredients in a bowl. Set aside.

Place the diced avocado, cucumber, cooled sweet potato, peas, spring onions and coriander in a serving bowl. Using your hands, toss gently to combine, being careful not to mush the avocado.

Drizzle over the dressing and toss again. Serve immediately.

HOT TIP If not serving straight away, I recommend keeping all the elements separate then bringing them together at the last minute, so everything can stay fresh, crunchy and delightful.

It's okay to put fruit in salad

PEACH, BUFFALO MOZ and JALAPEÑO SALAD with

MINT CHIMICHURRI

As far as summer salads go, this one is peaking. The sweetness of yellow peaches, the creaminess of mozzarella, the tang and fresh hit of mint chimichurri – it's so quick to throw together and so damn good to eat.

If you don't want to spend a mortgage repayment on fresh mozzarella, this also works really well with a Persian-style feta.

For forward planners, you can make the chimichurri the day before for a blink-and-you'll-miss-it assembly. It also has partner-in-crime-with-your-Christmas-ham written all over it, and it has never met a grilled protein it doesn't like. It's a salad for the ages. Just saying.

4–5 yellow peaches, washed

a little lemon or lime juice

2 balls (approx. 250 g/9 oz) buffalo mozzarella at room temperature (cold cheese is a crime)

½–1 jalapeño, seeds removed and very finely sliced

a few mint leaves, to serve

MINT CHIMICHURRI

1 cup mint leaves

juice of 1 lime

1 cup flat-leaf (Italian) parsley leaves

2 garlic cloves, peeled, chopped

½ tablespoon Turkish red pepper flakes

pinch of caster (superfine) sugar

pinch of sea salt flakes

50–125 ml (1¾–4 fl oz/¼–½ cup) good-quality olive oil

SERVES 4 AS PART OF A SPREAD

Cut your peaches into even slices, discarding the stones. Squeeze a little lemon or lime juice over your peach slices to prevent browning.

To make the mint chimichurri, place the ingredients in a food processor and blitz briefly to combine – you don't want to turn this into a uniform paste. Add more olive oil as needed.

Tear the mozzarella and spread across the base of a serving plate. Top with the peach slices, sliced jalapeño and torn mint leaves. Spoon over some chimichurri to taste and finish with a seasoning of olive oil, sea salt flakes and freshly ground black pepper.

Day of good intentions salad

CABBAGE and KALE SLAW WITH CHILLI, YEAST and SEED DRESSING

The benefit of this salad, other than its minimal preparation and amazing flavours, is its capacity to withstand not only time in the fridge but time on the table under our relentless summer heat.

1 large bunch cavolo nero (Tuscan kale), stems removed

¼ small white cabbage, external leaves removed

1 cup mint leaves, tightly packed, chopped

1 red chilli, seeds removed, finely sliced

DRESSING

125 g (4½ oz) pepitas (pumpkin seeds)

1 garlic clove, peeled, chopped

½ tablespoon oyster sauce (or use mushroom sauce to keep it vegan)

40 g (1½ oz/⅔ cup) nutritional yeast flakes

generous amount of olive oil, say 125–200 ml (4–7 fl oz/½–¾ cup)

generous pinch of sea salt flakes

SERVES 4 AS PART OF A SPREAD

Roll up the cavolo nero leaves and finely slice, then place in a bowl. If you have several large leaves, squeeze over some lemon juice; this will slightly soften the leaves, making them easier to chew and digest.

Finely slice the cabbage and mint and add them to the bowl. Add the chilli and toss to combine.

To make the dressing, add all the ingredients to a food processor and pulse briefly. You want this dressing to have a rough, pesto-like consistency. If it seems too thick, thin it out with some additional olive oil. Scoop this crunchy goodness over the slaw and toss with a couple of forks to combine. Check for seasoning and serve.

Salad like you mean it

SWEET POTATO, KALE and BURGHUL SALAD with CHERMOULA CASHEW DRESSING

This is a year-round salad. Serve it cold in summer and warm in the depths of winter. It is a moody salad with depth and heft but the shining star is that dressing. It is chef's kiss every. Single. Time.

1 kg (2 lb 3 oz) sweet potato, peeled and cut into bite-sized cubes

3–4 tablespoons olive oil

375 ml (12½ fl oz/1½ cups) chicken stock

200 g (7 oz) burghul (bulgur wheat)

1 small bunch cavolo nero (Tuscan kale), thick stems removed

1 large bunch coriander (cilantro), leaves and partial top of stems, chopped

CHERMOULA CASHEW DRESSING

leaves of 1 large bunch coriander (cilantro)

juice of 1 lime

80 ml (2½ fl oz/⅓ cup) olive oil

250 g (9 oz/1 cup) cashew butter

1 tablespoon soy sauce

SERVES 4

Preheat the oven to 180°C (360°F).

Spread the sweet potato over a baking tray lined with baking paper. Drizzle with the olive oil and roast for 30–40 minutes or until cooked through and looking nicely caramelised. Allow to cool.

To make the dressing, blitz all the ingredients, along with 2 tablespoons water, in a food processor to combine. If it seems too thick, add more water a tablespoon at a time. Season and set aside.

Bring the stock to a boil in a medium saucepan and add the burghul, cooking over a medium–high heat until tender (2–3 minutes). Drain well and spread over a tray to cool.

Finely slice the cavolo nero. If you have a lot of mature leaves, it can help to massage in a little lemon juice to soften.

Combine the sweet potato, burghul, cavolo nero and chopped coriander in a large bowl. Add just enough dressing to coat, erring on the side of caution. Turn onto a serving plate and then drizzle over a little extra dressing. Season with sea salt flakes and freshly ground black pepper and serve.

FRIED CAPER and ROAST CAPSICUM PANZANELLA

Bread. In a salad. The world makes sense after all. This is given a bit extra with all the salty, briny, crispy goodness of fried capers and the soft, earthy tang of roasted capsicum.

2–3 red capsicums (bell peppers), seeds removed, chopped into large chunks

2 tablespoons each red-wine vinegar, olive oil and brown sugar

1 small loaf sourdough, torn into chunks, crusts included

80–120 ml (2½–4 fl oz) olive oil, extra (or enough to coat the bread chunks)

3–4 large heirloom tomatoes, cut horizontally into thick, even slices

1 large bunch basil, leaves picked and torn

1–2 balls burrata (250–300 g/ 9–10½ oz) (or whatever cheese you have on hand that is easily breakable)

DRESSING

60 ml (2 fl oz/¼ cup) caramelised balsamic vinegar

60 ml (2 fl oz/¼ cup) olive oil

FRIED CAPERS

3 tablespoons olive oil

30 g (1 oz) capers

8–10 caperberries

SERVES 6 AS PART OF A SPREAD

Preheat the oven to 150°C (300°F).

Place the capsicum, red-wine vinegar, olive oil and brown sugar in a large roasting tin and toss to coat. Pop in the oven and roast until soft and caramelised, about 45 minutes. For the last 10 minutes of cooking, add the bread chunks and additional olive oil.

To make the dressing, combine the ingredients in a bowl, season to taste with sea salt flakes and set aside.

For the fried capers, place a frying pan over a medium heat and add the olive oil. Once hot, add the capers and caperberries. Fry until the capers look crisp and the caperberries have taken on some colour.

To serve, layer the heirloom tomato slices on a serving platter. Generously season with sea salt flakes and freshly ground black pepper. Use your hands to gently toss the capsicums and bread with the basil leaves then spoon over the tomato layer. Tear over the burrata and then spoon over the fried capers and caperberries. Finish by drizzling over the dressing and adding a generous seasoning of sea salt flakes and freshly ground black pepper.

IF YOUR FAFF FACTOR IS LOW Use jarred peppers and ditch roasting the capsicums.

KEEPING IT CHEAP AND CHEERFUL Swap out heirloom tomatoes for chuck tomatoes, ditch the caperberries and swap burrata for an economical soft cheese.

MAKE IT EXTRA Add basil flowers, micro basil and a mix of tomatoes on the vine with the heirlooms.

More is more

RANCHY CUKES and CRUNCHY BITS

Creamy, fresh, crunchy: all my salad ideals in one. Double batch the herby ranch. This is the kind of dressing you always want more of – it's so good you could drink it.

3–4 cukes, thinly sliced

2–3 continental cucumbers, thinly sliced

2 tablespoons sesame seeds

CRUNCHY RICE

120–160 ml (4–5½ fl oz) grapeseed oil

60 g (2 oz/⅓ cup) wild rice

QUICK HERBY RANCH DRESSING

125 g (4½ oz/½ cup) Kewpie mayonnaise

2 tablespoons honey mustard

50 ml (1¾ fl oz) buttermilk

1 tablespoon oyster sauce

½ large bunch basil, leaves picked (with a few reserved for serving)

SERVES 4 AS PART OF A SPREAD

To make the crunchy rice, place the oil in a saucepan over a high heat. Once the oil is very hot and shimmering, add the wild rice. Shake the pan constantly – the rice will puff and you will see flecks of white as it pops – about 10–15 seconds. As soon as this happens, strain the rice and then vigorously shake the strainer to remove any excess oil. Set the puffed rice aside until ready to serve.

To make the quick herby ranch dressing, add all the ingredients to a blender and give it a quick whizz until the basil has broken down into glorious little green flecks. It doesn't take much. Taste and season with sea salt flakes and freshly ground black pepper.

Put the sliced cucumbers in a bowl and drizzle over the ranch. This is a play-by-your-feelings situation. Toss to coat. Taste. If you want more dressing, keep going, or leave it with a light coating.

Transfer to a serving bowl and scatter over the extra basil leaves, then spoon over the crunchy rice and sesame seeds.

Season again with sea salt flakes and freshly ground black pepper and serve.

HOT TIP Leftover dressing spun through tinned smoked tuna and some chopped cos (romaine) then topped with a packet of sweet potato crisps is truly the five-second leftovers lunch of champions. Creamy, smoky, fresh and crunchy. Look at us, winning at life.

Clickbait

A VERY GOOD-LOOKING DINNER KIND OF SALAD

Bulky, delicious and with serious holding power, this is a meal kind of salad. There's so much textural interplay between the chewy grains, the freshness of the greens, the richness of the dates and then the heck yes! crunch of the nuts on top. I learnt the method for creating the shiny exterior on these nuts from a Danielle Alvarez cookbook. She tosses nuts in a sugar water laced with spices, then roasts them in the oven and they come out coated in crunch and gloss and are completely addictive. This is my interpretation.

If you get asked to bring a salad, this is what you bring.

190 g (6½ oz/1 cup) freekeh

2½ cups cavolo nero (Tuscan kale) leaves, large stems removed, finely sliced

115 g (4 oz/1½ cups) finely sliced red cabbage

160 g (5½ oz/1 cup) pitted dried dates, sliced

TAHINI CUMIN DRESSING

2 tablespoons olive oil

2 anchovy fillets

1 garlic clove

1 tablespoon tahini

juice and zest of ½ lemon

1½ teaspoons ground cumin

2 tablespoons honey mustard

½ cup freshly grated parmesan

2–3 tablespoons iced water

SWEET AND SALTY NUTS

30 g (1 oz) caster (superfine) sugar

1½ tablespoons olive oil

160 g (5½ oz) mixed raw nuts

100 g (3½ oz/⅔ cup) smoked almonds

generous pinch of sea salt flakes and cracked black pepper, to taste

½ teaspoon each ground cumin and ground coriander

½ teaspoon sweet smoked paprika

SERVES 4–6

To make the dressing, add all the ingredients to a food processor and blitz to combine. If it seems a little thick, add more water a tablespoon at a time until you achieve a dressing-like consistency.

Preheat your oven to 165°C (330°F).

For the sweet and salty nuts, place the water, sugar and olive oil in a small saucepan. Bring to a boil and cook until the sugar has dissolved, about 1 minute. Place the nuts on a tray lined with baking paper and pour over the sugar liquid, stirring to coat. Season with sea salt flakes and freshly ground black pepper. Bake for 22 minutes, stirring halfway through, until the nuts are roasted and fragrant. Pop the nuts into a mixing bowl with the spices and toss to coat. Allow to cool.

Cook the freekeh according to packet instructions and allow to cool. Combine in a bowl with the cavolo nero, red cabbage and dates. Drizzle over some of the dressing, just enough to lightly coat. Turn out into a large salad bowl, drizzle over the extra dressing and top with the nuts. Season with sea salt flakes and cracked black pepper and serve.

Chez, 'You've got this!'

QUICK FALAFEL 'n' GREENS SALAD

Green, crunchy, fresh and easy. I love this for its throw-together nature and robustness, making it perfect lunch fodder for work the next day. It's multi-use in that I'd happily call this dinner or let it share the table with all manner of proteins.

Preheat the oven to 160°C (320°F). Spread falafels on a tray and warm through in the oven, around 15–20 minutes.

To make the dressing, add all the ingredients to a food processor along with 125 ml (4 fl oz/½ cup) water and give a whirl to combine. If it seems thick, add a splash more water. It should look bright and green and fresh. Season with sea salt flakes and freshly ground black pepper.

Combine the salad ingredients in a bowl, tossing to combine. Add half the dressing and toss again to coat. Add a little more if you feel it's not coating the cabbage sufficiently. Turn out onto a serving plate and top with the falafels torn coarsely into bite-sized chunks, then drizzle over any remaining dressing. Season with sea salt flakes and freshly ground black pepper and serve.

200 g (7 oz) store-bought falafels

SALAD

½ small sugarloaf cabbage, finely sliced

1 bunch broccolini, finely sliced

leaves of 1 large bunch mint, finely sliced

1–2 teaspoons za'atar

100 g (3½ oz/¾ cup) dried cranberries

DRESSING

juice and zest of 1 lemon

80 ml (2½ fl oz/⅓ cup) olive oil

1–2 garlic cloves, chopped

1 cup fresh herbs (I use at least ½ cup mint, plus coriander/ (cilantro), flat-leaf/Italian parsley and dill)

3 tablespoons tahini

SERVES 4

The stuff of myths and legends

PUMPKIN and SOBRASADA SALAD with HOT HONEY FETA DRESSING

This salad is punchy and glorious and ridiculously simple to make. If our busy-life moniker is all about low effort, and high reward, you need this on rotation.

Sobrasada is a spicy spreadable sausage that's similar to chorizo but with a headier combination of spices. If you can't get your hands on any, replace with more spicy chorizo.

1 kent pumpkin (winter squash), skin on, sliced into even wedges, seeds removed

3 tablespoons olive oil

1 tablespoon sobrasada

1–2 chorizo sausages, skin removed, meat roughly chopped

4 very generous handfuls baby spinach leaves (like you are throwing confetti at a wedding)

leaves of 1 large bunch basil

fresh honeycomb, to serve (optional)

HOT HONEY AND FETA DRESSING

2 tablespoons olive oil

3 tablespoons honey (smoked if available)

120 g (4½ oz/½ cup) Persian feta

SERVES 4

Preheat the oven to 180°C (360°F).

Place the pumpkin in a roasting tin lined with baking paper. Drizzle over the olive oil and season generously with sea salt flakes and freshly ground black pepper. Roast for 45 minutes or until the pumpkin is tender and golden. Remove and set aside.

While the pumpkin is cooking, make the dressing. Add all the ingredients to a small saucepan and place over a medium heat. Cook, stirring regularly, until the feta has melted and everything is well combined and set aside.

Place a frying pan over a medium heat. Add the sobrasada and chorizo and cook, breaking up clumps with your wooden spoon, until the oil released is a lovely red golden colour and the meat has cooked through.

To serve, add the pumpkin, spinach leaves and basil to a large serving platter. Using your hands, give everything a gentle toss to combine. Spoon over the sobrasada mixture. If your dressing was made ahead, briefly reheat on a low heat in the saucepan then drizzle over the top of the salad. Season with sea salt flakes and freshly ground black pepper, then top with a cube of fresh honeycomb, if using.

Spankingly good salad
SPICY WATERMELON and CHUNKY CUKES SALAD

If summer was a salad, this would be it. Sweet, spicy, crunchy and tangy, with an ever-so-slightly lip-tingling chaser to make you feel alive. This is exactly what you should eat after a solid beach morning with sand still between your toes (and in your swimmers) and salt in your hair. And while we are continuing our idyllic beachside fantasy, this can be bulked out beautifully with some freshly barbecued prawns. Heaven-sent.

My only advice? Don't be shy and really get your spoon in there. That dressing liquid quietly gathering strength in the bottom of the bowl is so good that it should come with an adults-only rating.

45 g (1½ oz /¼ cup) brown sugar

2–3 tablespoons crunchy chilli oil (these vary in heat, so add one tablespoon at a time and taste)

75 g (2¾ oz/½ cup) pepitas (pumpkin seeds)

55 g (2 oz/½ cup) fried shallots

4–6 cups cubed watermelon (approx. 1.2 kg/2 lb 10 oz)

2 cups chunkily cut telegraph (long) cucumbers

2 spring onions (scallions), green part only, finely sliced

30 g (1 oz/1 cup loosely packed) coriander (cilantro) leaves

lime juice, to serve

DRESSING

60 ml (2 fl oz/¼ cup) lime juice

55 g (2 oz/¼ cup) brown sugar

1 tablespoon rice vinegar

1 tablespoon fish sauce

SERVES 4 AS PART OF A MEAL

Preheat the oven to 120°C (250°F).

Put the brown sugar, crunchy chilli oil and 4 tablespoons water in a small saucepan over a low heat. Simmer until the sugar has dissolved, stirring constantly. Spread the pepitas and fried shallots on a baking tray lined with baking paper and pour over the sugar and crunchy chilli mixture. Toss to combine. Pop in the oven for anywhere between 15 and 25 minutes – you want it to be golden and the liquid coating reduced so you have glossy, crunchy-looking pepitas. Remove and set aside while you assemble the salad.

Place the cut watermelon and cucumbers in a serving bowl. Scatter over the spring onions and coriander leaves and give everything a gentle toss with your hands.

Make the dressing by whisking all the ingredients in a bowl to dissolve the sugar. Pour the dressing over the watermelon and cucumber mixture. Top liberally with some of the crunchy pepita mixture. Give everything a good squeeze of lime juice and serve immediately. I like to serve any extra pepita mixture alongside – people are always going in for more.

Hells yes kind of salading
TURMERIC LEMONGRASS COLD NOODLE SALAD

600 g (1 lb 5 oz) wide
hand-pulled dried noodles

1 tablespoon sesame oil

2½ cups mixed soft herbs such
as mint, coriander (cilantro),
Thai basil, Vietnamese mint

LEMONGRASS AND TURMERIC DRESSING

1 tablespoon sesame oil

½ cup finely diced lemongrass
(white part only)

juice and zest of 3 limes

75 g (2¾ oz) salted roasted
cashews

½ tablespoon ground turmeric

6 makrut lime leaves, veins removed

¼ cup firmly packed coriander
(cilantro) leaves

1 garlic clove

2 tablespoons freshly grated ginger

3 tablespoons palm sugar

2 tablespoons fish sauce

pinch of chilli flakes or 1 fresh
red chilli, seeds removed,
finely chopped (optional)

TO SERVE

1 generous handful salted roasted
cashews

½ cup fried shallots

1–2 makrut lime leaves,
veins removed, finely sliced

SERVES 6–8
AS PART OF A SPREAD

This dressing, oh my lordy, I could drink it.
If this was the very last recipe of mine you
ever tried, I would rest my head and sleep
like a baby, safe in the knowledge of this
guaranteed flavour bomb.

It should be made in triple batches and kept
in the fridge to be called upon at a moment's
notice. As well as being noodles' perfect
partner, this dressing is glorious over a piece
of grilled fish or any protein you choose to
blanket in it.

If you purchase makrut lime leaves for this
recipe and have leftovers, they last
marvellously in the freezer, so never let them
get slowly mouldy in the back of the crisper.

I use wide hand-pulled noodles for this
recipe – they are my absolute favourite.
You can get a giant box from Costco – it's
a real bang for your buck situation.

To make the lemongrass and turmeric dressing, place all of the
ingredients in a food processor and blitz to an ever-so-slightly chunky
dressing consistency. If you feel it's too thick, thin out with a splash of
water. You can make this in advance as it will sit happily in the fridge
for a day or three. Just hide the spoons.

Cook the noodles according to the packet instructions. Strain and
immediately drizzle over the sesame oil (or more as needed) to
eliminate any concern over sticky noodles. Gently turn the noodles
with tongs to separate and coat in the oil, then set aside to cool for
5–10 minutes.

Once cooled, add the noodles to a bowl with all the fresh herbs and
give a gentle toss to combine. Turn out onto a serving platter and
drizzle at will with the dressing – you don't want to drown the noodles
in it, but its presence must be felt. Top with the salted cashews, fried
shallots and finely sliced makrut lime leaves.

Serve to applause.

HOT TIP This dressing is also great dolloped across
an omelette or smeared across a piece of salmon.
It really is the gift that keeps on giving.

MAKING FRIENDS WITH SALAD

Pretty much a cupboard salad

WHITE BEAN and COUSCOUS SALAD with ROASTED RED PEPPER DRESSING

Like olive oil, garlic and lemons, jarred peppers are an absolute workhorse in a busy kitchen. Adding instant packed earthy flavour and vibrant colour, a jar from your local supermarket for situations such as this is time and budget gold.

225 g (8 oz/1½ cups) wholemeal pearl couscous

1 × 400–420 g (14–15 oz) tinned white beans, drained and washed thoroughly

15 g (½ oz/¼ cup) spring onions (scallions), chopped

1 cup chopped mixed soft herbs such as dill, coriander (cilantro), parsley

juice of ½ lemon

2 tablespoons olive oil, plus extra to serve

180 g (6½ oz) haloumi, cut into even slices

ROASTED RED PEPPER DRESSING

2 large jarred roasted red peppers, rinsed

60 ml (2 fl oz/¼ cup) olive oil

3 tablespoons sherry vinegar

1 tablespoon caster (superfine) sugar

2 garlic cloves, chopped

SERVES 4

Cook the couscous according to the packet instructions. Strain and allow to cool slightly before placing in a bowl with the white beans, spring onions, chopped herbs and lemon juice. Add 1 tablespoon of the oil and stir to prevent sticking – there is something about clumps of pearl couscous that hang about in the back of your throat like the remnants of a bad cold.

Place a frying pan over a medium heat. Add the remaining olive oil and fry the haloumi slices until golden on both sides. Chop into bite-sized pieces and add to the bowl.

To make the dressing, place all the ingredients in a blender and give a quick blitz until combined and you have a dressing consistency. Season with some sea salt flakes and freshly ground black pepper.

Give the salad a little lug of extra olive oil to season and toss to combine. Turn out onto a serving plate and drizzle over the red pepper dressing. Season with sea salt flakes and freshly ground black pepper and serve.

A simple plate of yum

BLACK BEAN and AVO SALAD with CURRY and CORIANDER BUTTERMILK DRESSING

The five-second salad. This is for the haven't-got-my-week/day/will-to-exist/where-are-the-passports-life together. It's flavour under pressure.

400 g (14 oz) tinned black beans, drained and rinsed thoroughly

1 bunch cavolo nero (Tuscan kale), large stems removed and finely sliced

leaves of 1 large bunch coriander (cilantro), chopped, stems reserved for another use

juice and zest of 1 lime

75 g (2¾ oz) pepitas (pumpkin seeds)

2 avocados, hulled and sliced

DRESSING

80 ml (2½ fl oz/⅓ cup) buttermilk

125 g (4½ fl oz/½ cup) Kewpie mayonnaise

1 tablespoon oyster sauce

15 g (½ oz/½ cup) coriander (cilantro) leaves

1 tablespoon Keen's curry powder

SERVES 4 WITH A BIT OF PROTEIN/SOMETHING ELSE PLONKED ON THE TABLE

For the dressing, put the ingredients in a food processor and give them a quick whizz to combine. If you use a different brand of curry powder, add ½ tablespoon first and taste. They can vary in strength across brands, so best to be conservative and add slowly so you don't ruin your dressing.

Add all the other ingredients except for the avocados to a bowl. Give them a gentle toss, then add the avocado and spoon over the dressing and serve.

MY NAME is KATRINA and I like MINCE

I can feel the collective eye roll of foodies everywhere, but mince is a dinnertime wonder. Mind-blowing, I know.

Mince, the dinnertime pariah of food snobs, is not in fact the eye fillet of paupers – it is simply a zinging mealtime marvel for one and all. Carefully seasoned and left to brown properly, mince can make for ridiculously good eating. You just need a little patience, some thoughtful additions and the very best quality meat.

I should warn you, though, there is no mince on toast or bolognese in these pages: this is a foray into mince in all its glory. And truth be told, you have your bolognese, and I have my bolognese, and never the two shall meet. It's safest that way.

Side note: I have strong opinions on where my mince comes from and it's meat freshly minced at your local butcher. It makes a world of difference, having the same price as your supermarket but with far less water and, most importantly, none of those weird mince worms you get cooking a batch of the supermarket vacced and packed stuff. Also, you get to support a small business while sorting your dinner, and that is probably the greatest win of all.

The following recipes are a few other mincey mealtime options to add to your midweek rotation. Where I can I've identified the make one, freeze one, or what steps can be done ahead of time to make that weekday sh*t show, well, a little bit less of a sh*t show.

Can't stop eating them
LAMB ARAYES
with
PICKLED ONIONS
and HARISSA

Pita is stuffed with lamb, spices, herbs and love, then given a tan in the frying pan before spending a wee bit of time in the oven for crispy, juicy dinnertime goodness. I like to stuff the pita into oblivion for no other reason than I am a woman of appetites, and sometimes those appetites make me do things. You cannot have one part of me without the other.

10 pita breads, halved

60 ml (2 fl oz/¼ cup) olive oil for the pan

QUICK SUMAC ONIONS

1 red onion, finely sliced

½ tablespoon sumac

60 ml (2 fl oz/¼ cup) apple-cider vinegar

3 tablespoons caster (superfine) sugar

STUFFING

1 kg (2 lb 3 oz) minced (ground) lamb

3 garlic cloves, crushed

¼ cup each chopped mint, parsley and coriander (cilantro) leaves

3 tablespoons olive oil

2 teaspoons each sumac, ground coriander and ground cumin

1 tablespoon brown sugar

1 large egg

sea salt flakes and freshly ground black pepper, to season

TO SERVE

yoghurt

chopped parsley

harissa paste (optional)

MAKES BETWEEN 8 AND 10 (DEPENDING ON THE SIZE OF YOUR PITA AND HOW MUCH YOU STUFF THEM)

Preheat the oven to 180°C (360°F).

Combine the quick sumac onions ingredients in a bowl and set aside.

Place the stuffing mixture ingredients in a bowl and, using your hands, massage well until fully incorporated. Season with sea salt flakes and freshly ground black pepper.

Very gently open each pita and stuff firmly with the lamb mixture.

Put a frying pan over a medium heat. Add the oil and, once hot, fry each pita, open section down first, for about 3 minutes until golden and crisp, then fry the sides for 1–2 minutes each. Place the pitas on a large roasting tin and pop in the oven for 10–12 minutes until the mince mixture has cooked through.

Transfer the tray straight to your kitchen bench or wherever you may be serving them. Top with yoghurt, parsley, harissa (if using) and the sumac onions. Be careful not to burn the top of your mouth.

HOT TIP Don't skip the quick pickled sumac onions – they really give these a little something-something.

If you are feeding those with a sense of adventure and thirst for heat, a good dose of chilli flakes or harissa through the mince mixture is an added bonus. But leave out as a condiment to add if you have a mixed bag of tastes to feed.

Everything I like to eat

LOADED PORK LAAB with optional EXTRA CRISPY BITS

Fact: if you want your kids to eat what you feel like eating, add a spring roll on top. Ditto for most adults. Just a couple and you'll have them wrapping their mouths around this juicy bomb of a delight in no time.

You can buy toasted ground rice from Asian grocers, but if you want to make your own, toast some glutinous rice in a pan with a few makrut lime leaves until lightly golden (watch it like a hawk – if it burns, it's all over) and then pulse in a food processor. It keeps in an airtight container in a dark corner of your cupboard for a few months.

1½ tablespoons palm sugar
(or brown sugar if unavailable)

3 tablespoons fish sauce

juice of 3 limes (or more to taste)

125 ml (4 fl oz/½ cup) chicken stock

500 g (1 lb 2 oz) minced (ground) pork

3 teaspoons freshly grated galangal

1 lemongrass stem, white part only, very finely grated

3 makrut lime leaves, deveined, very finely sliced

45 g (1½ oz/¼ cup) toasted ground rice

3–5 dried chillies to taste

½ cup each chopped mint and coriander (cilantro) leaves

TO SERVE

lime wedges

extra chopped mint and coriander (cilantro) leaves

a few sneaky spring rolls

1 small sugarloaf cabbage, cut into wedges

fried shallots

raw green beans

SERVES 4

Combine the palm sugar, fish sauce and lime juice in a bowl and set aside for the sugar to dissolve.

In a non-stick frying pan over a medium heat, bring the chicken stock to a soft boil, then add the pork, galangal, lemongrass and makrut lime leaves. With a large metal spoon, work quickly to toss the pork so it cooks evenly (3–4 minutes). Once cooked through thoroughly and you can't see a single pink bit, remove from the heat. This is the trigger point: you want it cooked through, but you also don't want to overcook it as the meat will become tough rather than spongy and yielding like a trampoline for your mouth.

Transfer the pork to a bowl and add the ground rice, dried chillies, chopped herbs and the dissolved palm sugar mixture. Toss gently to incorporate. Taste and adjust seasoning – it should be spicy, sour and salty with just a slight hint of sweetness.

Serve with all the extras, and don't forget the spring rolls.

HOT TIP If you need to extend this to feed more mouths, serve with some steamed rice (and probably a few extra spring rolls).

It'll never let you down
A PIMPIN PICADILLO

I am relatively late to the picadillo party, but this great dish of both Spanish and Cuban roots is a dinner deal done right. I adore the sweetness of the raisins against the saltiness of the olives. This is absolutely a make one, freeze one situation, so double the quantity below. Your future self will thank you.

3–4 tablespoons olive oil

1 brown onion, diced

1 chorizo sausage, skin removed, meat chopped

4 garlic cloves, finely chopped

1 red capsicum (bell pepper), diced

1 red chilli, seeds removed and finely chopped

500 g (1 lb 2 oz) minced (ground) beef

500 g (1 lb 2 oz) minced (ground) pork

100 g (3½ oz/¾ cup) golden raisins

1 cup green olives, pitted

½ tablespoon each ground cumin and ground cinnamon

3 bay leaves

½ tablespoon dried oregano

2 × 790 g (1 lb 12 oz) tins crushed tomatoes

250 ml (8½ fl oz/1 cup) red wine

steamed rice, to serve

SERVES 6–8

Place a large deep-sided frying pan over a medium–high heat. Add olive oil and, once shimmering, fry the onions, chorizo and garlic, stirring regularly until the onions have started to soften and the chorizo juices have stained everything a muddy red colour.

Add the capsicum and chilli and cook for a few minutes or until softened. Add the beef and pork and allow it to brown. Try not to stir too much – you want this to caramelise and char a little in spots. Season with sea salt flakes and freshly ground black pepper.

Add the remaining ingredients, turn the heat to low and let the stew simmer for about an hour, longer if time allows. Season to taste and serve with steamed rice. I prefer a brown basmati because I am addicted to the slightly nutty taste and coarser texture.

Let's make meatloaf great again

GOCHUJANG HONEY MEATLOAF with FRIED SHALLOT CRUNCH

It's time we embraced meatloaf again. What was huge in the seventies became some culinary atrocity whispered about in dark corners for fear of admitting we still didn't mind participating in the odd loaf. I get it: many meals of my childhood involved eating Aberdeen sausage, meatloaf's awkward bready Scottish cousin – you know, the one no one really wanted to invite to the party but felt they had to. But this meatloaf, my fine friends, is a spot of mincey baked mastery. It's hot and cheesy and so bloody flavoursome. And the little one-two crunch for the finish is the stuff of legend. It's time for a comeback. And this should lead the charge.

splash of olive oil

3 red onions, diced

200 g (7 oz) smoky bacon, chopped

500 g (1 lb 2 oz) minced (ground) beef

500 g (1 lb 2 oz) minced (ground) pork

90 g (3 oz/¼ cup) honey

90 g (3 oz/1 cup) fresh sourdough breadcrumbs

3 tablespoons gochujang paste

180 g (6½ oz) cheddar cheese, cubed

fried shallots, to serve

GLAZE

90 g (3 oz/¼ cup) honey

1 tablespoon gochujang paste (or to taste)

150 ml (5 fl oz) barbecue sauce

SERVES 8–10

Preheat the oven to 180°C (360°F).

Add olive oil to a frying pan and, once hot, cook the onion until starting to soften. Add the bacon and cook for another 5 minutes or until the bacon looks nice and crisp.

Scrape into a bowl and let it cool before adding the remaining meatloaf ingredients.

Get your hands in there and mash everything together – you want the ingredients to be fully incorporated for an even loaf. Season generously with sea salt flakes and freshly ground black pepper.

Line a loaf tin with baking paper and make sure there is plenty of overhang for lifting this puppy out later. Firmly press the mixture into the base of the tin and try not to have any bits of cheese poking out as these tend to leach out while it cooks, and you want to capture that goodness. Ensure you have pressed down firmly so it holds its shape. Put in the oven and cook for 30 minutes.

While it is cooking, make the glaze by putting all the ingredients in a saucepan and bring to a simmer and cook until thickened, being careful not to let it burn.

After the loaf has cooked for 30 minutes, use the overhanging sheets of baking paper to transfer the meatloaf onto a lined baking tray. Pour three-quarters of the glaze over the top, letting some of it ooze down the sides; this will just add impact later. Return to the oven for another 45 minutes.

Remove from the oven and set aside to rest for 5 minutes before slathering it in as many fried shallots as you like. Carve into slices and scoop up any wayward saucy bits from the tray and spoon over the top. Serve with the remaining sauce.

Tuesday night taste of the exotic
STAR ANISE CHICKEN

I love this. It's exactly as I like to eat – plates of things to build many other great things. Bonus points if you can serve via a lazy Susan.

This is a riff on a far fancier braised chicken dish by icon Belinda Jeffery, but here I've made it with weeknight intent.

If you can handle the forward planning, chicken thighs minced freshly by a butcher will see this one really zing.

1 tablespoon grapeseed or other flavourless oil

1 kg (2 lb 3 oz) minced (ground) chicken

SAUCE

125 ml (4 fl oz/½ cup) kecap manis

125 ml (4 fl oz/½ cup) soy sauce

2 tablespoons oyster sauce

125 ml (4 fl oz/½ cup) chicken stock (or water)

30 g (1 oz) brown sugar

2–3 star anise

3 garlic cloves, crushed

2 tablespoons freshly grated ginger

SERVING IDEAS

1–2 baby cos (romaine) lettuce, washed, trimmed and leaves separated

steamed rice

1–2 cucumbers, chopped

bean sprouts

pickled ginger

fried vermicelli noodles for crunch

fresh mint and coriander (cilantro) leaves

SERVES 4–6

Throw the sauce ingredients in a saucepan and give them a quick stir. Pop over a medium–low heat and simmer for about 15 minutes until the sauce looks slightly reduced, glossy and thickened.

Place a frying pan over a medium heat. Add the oil and, once hot, add the chicken and stir regularly until browned and mostly cooked through. Pour over the reduced sauce and cook for an additional 5–10 minutes. You want the sauce to reduce further and coat the chicken.

Spoon the chicken onto a large serving platter. Serve any extras alongside so there is a glorious menagerie of fresh and vibrant ingredients to pile onto lettuce leaves and eat with joy.

MY NAME IS KATRINA AND I LIKE MINCE

Ball tearer

LAMB MEATBALLS
with five-second
ROMESCO
and HERBY FENNEL SLAW

Nothing irks me more than a broken meatball. Now I don't want to blow your mind here but we are going to embrace the reverse-sear methodology usually reserved for high-end cuts of meat for our wee little balls. Such a small hack, but so completely life-changing. They won't break, and they won't be black on the outside and raw in the middle – they will be soft and yielding in parts and crisp and caramelised in others. In other words, perfect.

FIVE-SECOND ROMESCO

2 jarred roasted red peppers

40 g (1½ oz/¼ cup) roasted cashews

1½ teaspoons sweet smoked paprika

1 garlic clove

grated zest of 1 lemon

olive oil as needed

MEATBALLS

60 g (2 oz/½ cup) pitted black olives, chopped

2 cups cavolo nero (Tuscan kale) leaves, finely sliced

4 garlic cloves

1 kg (2 lb 3 oz) minced (ground) lamb

2 slices bread soaked in 60 ml (2 fl oz/¼ cup) milk

110 g (4 oz/¾ cup) crumbled feta

TO SERVE

1 large bulb fennel, trimmed, bulb finely sliced, fronds reserved

basil and coriander (cilantro) leaves

lemon juice

170 g (6 oz) yoghurt

SERVES 8

Preheat the oven to 150°C (300°F).

Make the five-second romesco by adding all the ingredients except the oil to a blender or food processor, give a quick whizz, then slowly pour in some olive oil as it churns until the ingredients come together and you have a mixture slightly thinner than hummus. Season generously with sea salt flakes and freshly ground black pepper and set aside.

Make the meatballs by putting all the ingredients in a bowl and getting your hands in there to evenly incorporate. Stop kneading as soon as the mixture feels sticky to the touch. Roll into meatballs about the size of golf balls.

Generously oil an ovenproof, non-stick frying pan. Add the balls and pop in the oven for 20 minutes. Remove (don't forget the handle is hot) and place over a medium heat. Allow the meatballs to brown, carefully turning to get an even tan on all sides. The meatballs are essentially already cooked, so this is just giving them that touch of crisp and colour. Like a small child in a pool, these shouldn't be left to their own devices. Keep an eye on them.

Make a quick salad by adding the fennel and herbs to a bowl. Squeeze over some lemon juice and toss gently to coat.

To serve, smear a plate with the romesco and top with the salad, meatballs and yoghurt. Season with sea salt flakes and freshly ground black pepper and finish with a generous lug of olive oil.

HOT TIP This makes more romesco than you need. (You're welcome.) Swipe leftovers on toast and top with eggs, or stir through pasta, or swap in for tomato sauce on a pizza base. Use it to glow up tomorrow's ham sandwich. Add some fontina for a cheese toastie for the ages.

Just so damn lovely ...

CRISPY CRUNCHY MOUSSAKA

I love moussaka, but where is the crunch? I've scrunched some filo pastry into oblivion to give this a pie vibe and everyone is winning. Smoky, creamy, crunchy, aka ultimate mealtime satisfaction.

I'll often double batch the sauce to speed up the midweek meal efficiency as it freezes like a dream, making this recipe more weekday friendly.

2–3 medium eggplants (aubergine) (approx. 800 g/1 lb 12 oz)

8–12 filo pastry sheets

plenty of melted butter for brushing

SAUCE

80 ml (2½ fl oz/⅓ cup) olive oil

2 red onions, finely diced

4 garlic cloves, crushed

1 teaspoon ground cinnamon

3 tablespoons finely chopped oregano

800 g (1 lb 12 oz) minced (ground) lamb

400 g (14 oz) tinned crushed tomatoes

325 ml (11 fl oz) red wine

300 ml (10 fl oz) chicken stock

1 bay leaf

salt and ground black pepper, to season

BECHAMEL

60 g (2 oz) salted butter

60 g (2 oz) plain (all-purpose) flour

425 ml (14½ fl oz) milk

2 garlic cloves, crushed

pinch of grated nutmeg

ground white pepper and sea salt flakes, to season

SERVES 6

Turn a barbecue hotplate to high. Grill the eggplants for 20–30 minutes, turning regularly so they char all over. You want to have genuine fear you'll burn the house down – they need to get white-hot and charred for the smoky flavour to translate to the final dish. Transfer to a colander in the sink and let the juices run. Once cool enough to handle, remove the skin and stem. Set aside the flesh.

Preheat the oven to 170°C (340°F).

For the sauce, add the oil to a large frying pan and place over a medium heat. Once hot, add the onions and cook for 2–3 minutes or until soft and translucent. Add the garlic, cinnamon and oregano and cook for another minute or until fragrant. Add the lamb in a lump like a large burger patty and allow it to brown on the edges before breaking it up with a spoon and cooking for another 5 minutes or until just cooked through. Add the remaining sauce ingredients, season with sea salt flakes and ground black pepper, and simmer for at least 20 minutes or until the sauce has reduced.

Make the bechamel by melting the butter in a saucepan over a low heat. Add the flour and cook for 1 minute, stirring constantly. Gradually add the milk, still stirring. Stir in the garlic then stir for 2–5 minutes until it thickens and coats the back of a wooden spoon. Remove from the stove and add the nutmeg and season with the white pepper and some sea salt flakes.

Add the eggplant flesh to the lamb mixture and stir to combine. I find adding it at the end retains more of the smoky flavour. If you love a really deep hit of smoke, you can also add a drop or two of liquid smoke.

Spoon the sauce into an ovenproof dish and then spoon over most of the bechamel, reserving about half a cup for the end of the dish.

Scrunch the filo pastry as if you were scrunching a sheet of newspaper to throw into a fire. Place the pastry sheets on top of the bechamel layer and brush generously with melted butter. If you have any gaps, this is where you pour in the last half cup of the bechamel, so it fills all the nooks and crannies.

Pop in the oven and cook for 30–40 minutes or until golden brown. Season with sea salt flakes and serve.

Satisfaction in a bowl

DONBURI BEEF with SAKE CUKES

When feeding is the order of the day. This could easily be in the SOS chapter if it weren't for the dashi, which is not in everyone's pantry, so it sits here instead. This one is so fast, it will take longer to cook the rice for serving.

My kids inhale this so it sits on high rotation when we just need to get dinner done.

Just leave the sake out of the cucumbers for little mouths ... or don't. No judgement here.

SAKE CUKES

1 telegraph (long) cucumber, sliced fairly thickly

125 ml (4 fl oz/½ cup) sake

3–4 tablespoons toasted mixed sesame seeds

BEEF

3 tablespoons olive oil

500 g (1 lb 2 oz) minced (ground) beef

2 tablespoons finely grated fresh ginger

125 ml (4 fl oz/½ cup) sake

80 ml (2½ fl oz/⅓ cup) dashi (or liquid kombu)

80 ml (2½ fl oz/⅓ cup) soy sauce

3 tablespoons brown sugar

1 cup green things – thawed frozen peas, edamame, fresh runner beans, chopped broc, whatever you have on hand will do

steamed rice, to serve

pickled ginger and sliced spring onions, to serve

SERVES 4-6

For the sake cukes, toss the cucumber slices and sake in a bowl. Sprinkle over the toasted sesame seeds and set aside.

Place a frying pan over a medium heat, add the oil and when it's hot and shimmering, add the beef in one lump. Press it down into the hot pan like a burger patty and let it get nice and caramelised. Grate the ginger right over the top and then give it a few turns, like you are flipping a burger, until the ginger is fragrant. Add the sake and let things get acquainted before adding the dashi, soy sauce and brown sugar. Start breaking up the meat with a spoon and let the sauce caramelise and reduce slightly, then add your greens and cook until just warmed through but still bright and fresh. Season to taste with sea salt flakes and freshly ground pepper.

Add rice to bowls. Top with the beef mixture, sake cukes and pickled ginger. Serve immediately.

The real MVP
BLOODY MARY'S BIG BALLS
with FRIED PICKLES

On most occasions, I think meatballs should be big 'n' juicy. They should be served standalone and enjoyed like the glorious vessels of good times that they are.

Also, we should all be frying our pickles. There are pickles, and then there are charred fried pickles. The end.

PS: I don't serve these on pasta *Lady and the Tramp* style, but I do love to serve something carb-adjacent for the full experience. A Bloody Mary for washdown isn't bad either if you really want to embrace the theme.

Double batch the sauce for life convenience then freeze some.

4 pita or a few pieces of white bread, coarsely torn

250 ml (8½ fl oz/1 cup) milk

60 g (2 oz/1 cup) dill leaves, chopped

500 g (1 lb 2 oz) minced (ground) pork

500 g (1 lb 2 oz) minced (ground) beef

4 garlic cloves, crushed

1 onion, finely diced

1 egg

½ tablespoon tomato paste (concentrated purée)

1 tablespoon sweet smoked paprika

½ tablespoon each celery seeds, ground coriander and ground cumin

generous glug of olive oil, for frying

sliced sweet and spicy pickles, to serve

SAUCY SAUCE

3 tablespoons olive oil

2 onions, chopped

6 garlic cloves

1 small stalk celery, finely diced

pinch of celery seeds

pinch of ground coriander

125 ml (4 fl oz/½ cup) sweet and spicy pickle juice

140 g (5 oz) tomato paste (concentrated purée)

120 ml (4 fl oz) vodka

2 tablespoons Worcestershire sauce

2 tablespoons brown sugar

½ cup sliced sweet and spicy pickles, chopped

700 ml (23½ fl oz) tomato passata (puréed tomatoes)

250 ml (8½ fl oz/1 cup) chicken stock

800 g (1 lb 12 oz) tinned crushed tomatoes

ROLLS 6 BIG ONES

To make the saucy sauce, place a stockpot over a medium-low heat. Add the oil and, once hot, fry the onions, garlic and celery until soft. Add the celery seeds and ground coriander and continue to cook until fragrant. Add the pickle juice and tomato paste and cook until the onion is coated in the mixture and has darkened in colour. Add the vodka, Worcestershire sauce, brown sugar and chopped pickles. Cook for 5 minutes or until slightly reduced and it looks nice and glossy. Add the passata, stock and tinned crushed tomatoes. Turn the heat to very low and let it simmer while you have a lie down for about an hour.

Preheat the oven to 170°C (340°F).

To make the balls, put the pita or bread in a bowl and pour over the milk. Set aside for 15 minutes or until softened. Add half the dill and the remaining ingredients to a large bowl, season with sea salt flakes and ground black pepper, and use your hands to roughly combine. Squeeze any excess milk from the pita or bread bits and add to the bowl, discarding the milk. Give everything a good mix with your hands. Take a hunk of mixture and roll into a ball about the size of a tennis ball – it should only just fit in your hands.

Place a frying pan over a low heat. Add the olive oil and, once hot, add the meatballs and gently fry on all sides, just to get a bit of colour. Be careful not to overcrowd the pan and squish them into oblivion; a gentle cook and turn is what is required here. Transfer to a large roasting dish and cover with the sauce, keeping the frying pan to the side. Pop in the oven and cook for 45 minutes, turning halfway through.

Just before they are ready, place the frying pan back on a medium heat. Add the sliced pickles and let them sizzle in the leftover pan juices until beginning to char. Keep an eye on them as this will vary between brands and the sugar content in the pickles. You want a lovely char, then flip and repeat.

Remove the meatballs from the oven and top with the fried pickles and remaining chopped dill. Season recklessly with sea salt flakes and cracked black pepper and serve.

Satay like you mean it

SATAY CHICKEN POP TARTS

Three of my favourite things. Pop tarts. Spring rolls. Anything satay.

1 tablespoon vegetable oil, plus extra for shallow-frying

2 garlic cloves, finely chopped

1 tablespoon finely grated ginger

400 g (14 oz) chicken thigh mince

2 teaspoons ground coriander

1 teaspoon each curry powder, ground cumin, ground turmeric, sea salt flakes and ground black pepper

¼ cup fried shallots

¼ cup smooth peanut butter

60 ml (2 fl oz/¼ cup) coconut milk

2 tablespoons soy sauce

8 large square spring roll wrappers (21 cm/8¼ in)

1 egg, lightly beaten

SATAY SAUCE

1 tablespoon excellent-quality red curry paste

50 g (1¾ oz) palm sugar (or brown sugar if unavailable)

1 tablespoon sweet soy sauce

½ tablespoon soy sauce

½ tablespoon lime juice

200 g (7 oz) smooth peanut butter

1 teaspoon fish sauce

1 tablespoon apple-cider vinegar

185 ml (6 fl oz/¾ cup) chicken stock

chopped slated peanuts, to serve

MAKES 8

Heat the oil in a large wok or frying pan over a high heat. Add the garlic and ginger and cook until fragrant, about 30 seconds. Add the chicken, spices and fried shallots and fry, breaking up the meat with the back of a wooden spoon until caramelised and cooked through. Combine the peanut butter, coconut milk and soy sauce in a bowl. Pour over the chicken mix and stir to combine. Continue to cook until the liquid is mostly absorbed (you don't want an overly wet mixture).

Working with one spring roll wrapper at a time, spoon ⅓ cup of the filling on one half, leaving a 1 cm (½ in) border. Brush the edge with the egg and fold over to seal. Repeat with the remaining wrappers and filling.

Fill a wok a third full with vegetable oil and place over a medium–high heat until the oil reaches 180°C (360°F). Working in batches, cook the pop tarts until golden and crisp (1–2 minutes), flipping regularly to crisp on all sides. Drain on paper towel and repeat with remaining pop tarts. These are best eaten immediately, but I have on occasion reheated them on a tray in the oven until crisp again and found them almost as delightful.

For the satay sauce, put all the ingredients in a saucepan and stir thoroughly. Place over a low heat and cook until the sauce thickens and is delightfully aromatic, about 5 minutes. If it gets too thick, thin out with stock or water.

Serve the pop tarts with the warm satay sauce for dipping and a smattering of chopped peanuts.

BIG
BOWLS
of
COMFORT

There is a definite place in the world for dishes that are emotional bandaids, and I like that place. You always know where you stand with comfort food, an eternally reliable salve that both soothes and satisfies.

While that idea of comfort is inherently personal, comfort food is childhood nostalgia, undiluted pleasure and the sort of foods that serve to blot out whatever may ail us, making our immediate world a much kinder place to reside in.

These are dishes to help us feel grounded and connected. There is love and care and joy in the cracks. Nothing fussy or complicated, these are earthy, robust and warm dishes, the sort of flavour combinations that make you feel as though life has linked arms with you and is again, at last, walking in step.

When only pasta will do
LAZY EGGPLANT PASTA with OLIVES

The kind of confident, nonchalant dish that makes your humble bolognese ache with jealousy. The roasted eggplant tomato concoction creates a damn fine sauce that slips and holds with the requisite tension we all require from our Tuesday night bowl of pasta.

1 large eggplant (aubergine), diced

1 whole bulb of garlic, unpeeled and halved

500 g (1 lb 2 oz) mixed medley cherry tomatoes

½ cup smoked semi-dried tomatoes

a few thyme sprigs to scatter

3 tablespoons olive oil

1 tablespoon brown sugar

2 tablespoons red-wine vinegar

500 g (1 lb 2 oz) bucatini pasta

TO SERVE

kalamata olives, pitted and chopped (bonus points if smoked)

pinch of chilli flakes

parmesan, finely grated

SERVES 4

Preheat the oven to 185°C (365°F).

Add the eggplant, garlic, tomatoes and thyme to a baking tray and drizzle with the olive oil, brown sugar and vinegar. Toss gently to coat. Roast for 45 minutes or until golden. When cool enough to handle, squeeze the garlic cloves from their skins and add the soft garlic and roasted vegetables to a blender, discarding the thyme stems. Blitz briefly while warm.

Bring a pot of well-salted water to a boil. Add the bucatini and cook for 10 minutes or until al dente. Reserve 500 ml (17 fl oz/2 cups) of the pasta water, then strain pasta and return to the pot.

Add 1 cup of the pasta water to the blitzed vegetables and blend until you have a smooth and creamy sauce. Add more from the additional cup of pasta water if you feel the sauce is too thick. Pour the sauce over the bucatini and use tongs to turn and coat.

Season generously and serve topped with chopped olives, chilli flakes and plenty of parmesan.

Soothing power

WEDNESDAY NIGHT CHICKEN SAAG

This is one that you crave. You'll be going about your day and then wham – life is incomplete without it. There is something about curry, with its domestic rituals of spice-roasting and layering of flavour, that is a balm for the soul. Add a heft of spinach, the green of a churning winter ocean after a storm, and this is a truly soothing dish, particularly when swept at with crispy, flaky pieces of hot naan.

My suggestion: eat with your eyes closed. Breathe. Enjoy the immediate and consuming comfort a dish like this brings. Serve with all the things – rice, roti, pappadums and wine for dinnertime nirvana.

---

300 g (10½ oz) baby spinach leaves

3 tablespoons ghee or flavourless oil

2 large onions, diced

6 garlic cloves, crushed

40 g (1½ oz) finely chopped ginger

800 g (1 lb 12 oz) chicken thighs, cut into chunks

3 teaspoons each ground coriander, garam masala, ground turmeric, ground cumin, ground cardamom and fenugreek seeds

pinch of chilli powder to taste

70 g (2½ oz) tomato paste (concentrated purée)

375 ml (12½ fl oz/1½ cups) chicken stock

300 ml (10 fl oz) pouring (single) cream or Greek-style yoghurt, plus extra to drizzle

SERVES 6

Place a large deep-sided frying pan over a medium heat. Add a tablespoon of water and the spinach and cook briefly until the spinach begins to wilt and dramatically reduce in size but still looks vibrant and green. Scoop into a food processor and give a quick blitz to combine. Set aside.

Add the ghee to the same frying pan and place over a low heat. Add the onions and cook until completely soft. It's important not to rush this step as it is where a lot of the flavour begins, so give it 10 minutes at least.

Add the garlic and ginger and cook until fragrant. Season with salt and push to the side of the pan. Add the chicken to the pan and cook for 2 minutes or until browned all over. Add the spices and chilli powder and stir to coat.

Add the tomato paste and stock and cook for another minute. Stir in the cream or yoghurt and cook for 20 minutes on low so the flavours can get acquainted (even longer if you have the patience). Stir through the spinach and cook for another few minutes. Taste and check for seasoning.

HOT TIP You can completely omit the chilli powder if feeding small people – it is still an excellent curry and super flavoursome.

One strong tip: freshly grind your spices where possible. Your future curry-eating self will thank you profusely.

KITCHEN KEEPERS   66

Everything is fine

PASTA with BUTTER-ROASTED TOMATO SAUCE and CACIO E PEPE CHICKPEAS

This is culinary magic with cupboard staples. Cheap, cheerful carbs that prove you can do a lot with a little.

500 g (1 lb 2 oz) of your favourite pasta

grated parmesan, to serve

BUTTER-ROASTED TOMATOES

3 × 400 g (14 oz) tins whole peeled tomatoes

8 garlic cloves

3 anchovy fillets

60 g (2 oz) salted butter

CACIO E PEPE CHICKPEAS

80 ml (2½ fl oz/⅓ cup) olive oil

400 g (14 oz) tinned chickpeas, drained and rinsed thoroughly

75 g (2¾ oz/¾ cup) finely grated parmesan

25 g (1 oz/¼ cup) finely grated pecorino

sea salt and freshly ground black pepper, to serve

SERVES 4–6

Preheat the oven to 200°C (390°F).

For the butter-roasted tomatoes, dump everything in an ovenproof dish, watching those splashy tinned tomatoes that seem to find a white t-shirt from 500 paces. Season with salt and a generous heft of freshly ground black pepper. Give everything a good stir, then pop in the oven to roast until the mixture is thick and reduced and smells like heaven, about 40 minutes.

While the tomatoes are roasting, make the cacio e pepe chickpeas. Place all the ingredients in a roasting tin lined with baking paper and season with freshly ground black pepper. Give it a good shake to coat and combine, then pop in the oven and cook until the chickpeas are crisp and golden, anywhere between 5 and 15 minutes depending on the spirit of your oven. Set aside.

Remove the butter-roasted tomatoes from the oven and, using a couple of forks, mash any larger tomatoes to help make the sauce.

Bring a large pot of water to a boil over a high heat and salt generously. Add the pasta and cook according to packet instructions. When cooked, scoop out 250 ml (8½ fl oz/1 cup) of pasta cooking liquid and add it to the tomato sauce mixture, giving everything a good stir, then drain the pasta. Add the pasta to the sauce and toss to combine. Season generously with salt, freshly ground black pepper and a few generous gratings of parmesan.

Scoop the pasta into bowls. Top with some cacio e pepe chickpeas and give everything a good smattering of sea salt flakes and a generous dose of ground black pepper and serve.

Oh darl ...
BUTTER DAL

I love butter chicken. I love dal. This is the moment those worlds collide and it's just beautifully excellent. An alchemy of needs. From me to you.

If you don't have panch phoron mix, you can easily and far more cheaply make your own by combining 1 teaspoon each of cumin, brown mustard, fenugreek, nigella and fennel seeds.

250 g (9 oz/1 cup) red lentils, rinsed well and drained

1 teaspoon ghee

1 French shallot, sliced

2 tablespoons panch phoron mix

BUTTER SAUCE

1 tablespoon ghee

1 red onion, diced

2 tablespoons finely chopped ginger

4 garlic cloves, chopped

2 teaspoons each sweet smoked paprika, ground cumin and ground turmeric

1 teaspoon each fennel seeds, fenugreek seeds and coriander seeds, toasted and ground

1½ tablespoons garam masala

1 tablespoon tomato paste (concentrated purée)

400 g (14 oz) tinned crushed tomatoes

150 ml (5 fl oz) vegetable stock

400 ml (13½ fl oz) pouring (single) cream or coconut cream

1 cinnamon stick

125 g (4½ oz) salted butter

TO SERVE

juice of 1 lime or lime wedges

yoghurt

hot, fluffy naan

chopped coriander

SERVES 4–6

To make the butter sauce, place a large frying pan over a medium heat. Add the ghee and, once hot, fry the onion until soft and translucent. Add the ginger and garlic and cook until fragrant before adding the spices and tomato paste. Cook until you can really smell those spices and the tomato paste appears to have come away from the pan and is sticking to your onion mix like glue while being slightly darkened in colour. Add the tomatoes and stock and bring to a simmer, cooking for about 15 minutes so your ingredients become friends.

Remove from the heat and stir through the cream. Allow to cool before transferring to a blender and blitzing to a smooth sauce. Pour that back into the pan and add your cinnamon stick and the butter. Simmer for 10 minutes before adding the washed lentils, then simmer again on a low heat for 20 minutes or until your lentils are cooked to your liking.

While the lentils are simmering, place a small frying pan over a medium heat. Add the teaspoon of ghee and fry the sliced French shallot until crisp and delightful. Transfer to a bowl and immediately add the panch phoron mix to the pan and cook for 30 seconds to 1 minute, or until you see the brown mustard seeds start to pop. Scrape onto the French shallots and stir to combine.

Spoon the dal into bowls and top with lime juice or wedges, some yoghurt, chopped coriander and the fried shallots mixture. Serve piping hot with naan.

Trust the tofu

MISO EGGPLANT of the GODS

My guiltiest pleasure is the eggplant donburi from my local takeaway joint, Uncle Don's, and this is my rendition. Even if it's not perfect, it's a quarter of the price. Even if you hate tofu (I understand, and you are seen), it makes the most luscious, creamiest goodness to drizzle over the top – you need to make it. And soon. With a real sense of urgency. It's that good.

2 eggplants (aubergines), sliced into about 1½ cm (½ in) rounds

sesame oil to drizzle

TOFU CREAM

155 g (5½ oz/1 cup) cashews

300 g (10½ oz) silken tofu

MARINADE

3 tablespoons caster (superfine) sugar

70 g (2½ oz) white miso paste

3 tablespoons mirin

3 tablespoons sake

TO SERVE

steamed rice of your choice (I love jasmine or brown basmati)

sliced spring onions (scallions)

furikake, if you have some, or roasted sesame seeds and chilli flakes

SERVES 4

Preheat your oven to 200°C (390°F).

To start the tofu cream, pop the cashews in a bowl and cover with some water.

Combine the marinade ingredients in a bowl and give a quick whisk so everything is properly incorporated. Set aside.

Spread the eggplant slices over a large baking tray lined with baking paper. Drizzle sparingly with sesame oil – it's for background flavour only. Roast for 20–25 minutes or until softened and cooked through.

Remove the tray from the oven and gently flip the pieces of eggplant. Spoon the marinade onto the eggplant circles. Turn your oven to the grill (broiler) function and pop the tray under it for a maximum of 2 minutes – watch carefully so they don't burn. Alternatively, if you have a blowtorch, it is amazing to torch the eggplants instead and add a gloriously smoky, charred element to the dish, not to mention the free therapy a little live burning achieves.

To finish the tofu cream, strain the cashews and blitz in a strong blender with the tofu until you have a beautiful creamy sauce. Season with a generous pinch of salt.

To serve, top rice with slices of caramelised eggplant. Drizzle over some of the tofu cream and top with spring onions, furikake (if using) or the chilli, sesame mix and spring onion. Season with salt flakes and serve immediately.

BIG BOWLS OF COMFORT

Takeaway dreams can come true

LEMON and HONEY CHICKEN

650 g (1 lb 7 oz) boneless, skinless chicken thighs

3–4 tablespoons rice bran oil or other flavourless oil

MARINADE

1 tablespoon sesame oil

juice of ½ lemon

1 teaspoon sea salt flakes

1 tablespoon caster (superfine) sugar

60 ml (2 fl oz/¼ cup) shaoxing rice wine

1 chicken stock (bouillon) cube, crumbled

½ teaspoon each ground cinnamon, ground fennel seeds and ground sichuan peppercorns

HONEY LEMON SAUCE

260 g (9 oz/¾ cup) honey

juice and zest of 2 lemons

2 tablespoons cornflour (cornstarch) mixed with a dash of water to make a slurry

TO SERVE

steamed white rice

1 spring onion (scallion), finely sliced

½ teaspoon roughly crushed sichuan peppercorns

1–2 tablespoons sesame seeds (white or black or both)

SERVES 4–6

Growing up, takeaway glory lived three blocks away at Seventh Heaven, an iconic (to me) suburban Chinese restaurant. The red-trimmed door led to one of the most glorious food memories of my childhood. I can still feel the questionably aged carpet under my feet and smell the oil licked by garlic and chilli. This recipe is an amalgamation of my childhood memories, with a wisp of sichuan peppercorns for mouth-warming heat and cut-through. It's sweet, sticky comfort in a bowl, perfect for midweek.

If you can't find sichuan peppercorns at your supermarket or Asian grocers, substitute with white pepper. It's worth looking though – there is really nothing like them.

Combine the marinade ingredients in a bowl, then add the chicken thighs and turn to coat well. If time is on your side, it's wondrous to marinate the chicken in the fridge overnight, but I've also done a quick dump and turn in the marinade and been just as happy. Either way, bring to room temperature before cooking.

To make the honey lemon sauce, put the honey and lemon juice and zest in a small saucepan over a medium heat. Cook, stirring to prevent catching, until the honey has warmed and the juice and zest are incorporated – it will begin to foam a little. Remove from the heat and stir through the cornflour slurry until combined. Return to the heat and continue to stir until the mixture is the thickness of golden syrup – you want it to still be runny but gloriously thick. Set aside until ready to serve.

Place a large non-stick frying pan over a medium–high heat. Add the rice bran oil and, once hot, fry the marinated chicken thighs until browned (2–3 minutes each side). Reduce the heat to medium and continue frying until cooked through, up to another 5–7 minutes depending on thickness.

While hot, transfer with tongs to a chopping board and slice the chicken thighs into bite-sized pieces. Put in a large bowl with the honey lemon sauce, gently turning to coat.

To serve, add chicken to bowls of steamed white rice and top with the sliced spring onions, crushed sichuan peppercorns and sesame seeds.

SPANAKORIZO with HALOUMI

The hidden veg bar has been raised

This traditional Greek dish is comfort personified. Its name is a composite of the two key ingredients: spanaki, meaning spinach, and rizi, meaning rice. What's missing in the literal definition is 'freaking delicious', which is exactly what this is.

Spanakorizo is the glory of spanakopita without the commitment of dealing with filo. And you can feel wholesome feeding a mass of greens to those you love. The slab of squeaky haloumi only adds to the appeal.

125 ml (4 fl oz/½ cup) olive oil, plus extra for the haloumi

6 spring onions (scallions), finely chopped

3 garlic cloves, grated

600 g (1 lb 5 oz) baby spinach (this seems like an awful lot but cooks down to nothing very rapidly)

200 g (7 oz/1 cup) long-grain rice, rinsed in cold water

½ cup chopped flat-leaf (Italian) parsley

1 litre (34 fl oz/4 cups) vegetable stock

225 g (8 oz) haloumi, evenly sliced

finely sliced lemon, to serve

fresh herbs and edible flowers to scatter (optional)

SERVES 4–6

Add the olive oil to a large deep-sided frying pan with a lid and place over a medium heat. Fry the spring onions and garlic, stirring constantly to prevent catching, until fragrant and soft. Add the spinach – it may seem like it won't fit, but just keep pushing it down as it will wilt and decrease in volume. Once completely wilted, stir through the rice and parsley, then pour over the stock. Cover and cook for 30 minutes on a low heat.

After 30 minutes, check to see if the rice is cooked. If it is but the liquid is still visible, continue to cook uncovered for a little longer. Remove from the heat and set aside uncovered for a few minutes before serving.

While the rice is resting, fry your haloumi in a frying pan with some olive oil until golden and crisp, about 1–2 minutes.

Spoon the rice into a large serving bowl. Top with the finely sliced lemon and the haloumi. Give everything a little drizzle of olive oil and season generously with sea salt flakes and freshly ground black pepper.

Dirty in a good way

DIRTY MARTINI CHICKEN THIGHS with BURST TOMATOES and FETA

When you want a dirty martini but it's Tuesday and you need to make dinner, this is your panacea.

It's the small victories.

2 tablespoons salted butter

2 tablespoons olive oil

6–8 chicken thighs, skin on

6 garlic cloves, finely chopped

60 ml (2 fl oz/¼ cup) gin

60 ml (2 fl oz/¼ cup) vermouth

790 g (1 lb 12 oz) tinned crushed tomatoes

1 tablespoon brown sugar

1 handful basil, finely chopped, plus whole leaves, extra, to serve

1 handful flat-leaf (Italian) parsley, finely chopped

1 cup pitted green olives, plus 125 ml (4 fl oz/½ cup) brining liquid

150 g (5½ oz/generous ½ cup) soft feta

1–2 stems (about 500 g/1 lb 2 oz) cherry tomatoes on the vine

SERVES 4–6

Preheat the oven to 175°C (345°F).

Place an ovenproof frying pan over a medium–low heat. Add the butter and oil and, once hot, fry the chicken thighs, skin side down, until the skin looks caramelised and crisp, around 10–15 minutes. Flip the chicken thighs skin side up and add the garlic to the pan. Simmer until fragrant then add the gin and vermouth. Cook until the booze has mostly reduced before adding the crushed tomatoes, brown sugar, herbs and olives. Top with pieces of the feta and the vine tomatoes and pop in the oven for 30 minutes.

Remove from the oven, season with sea salt flakes and freshly ground black pepper, top with the whole basil leaves and serve.

LULU'S SUNDAY NIGHT HONEY MUSTARD CHICKEN DRUMSTICKS

My daughter is obsessed with honey mustard. She is constantly looking for ways to use it so she can eat it at every opportunity. This is her kid-in-the-kitchen chicken, and it has low-key Sunday night vibes written all over it – easy, finger-licking deliciousness. Kid-approved.

250 ml (8½ fl oz/1 cup) chicken stock

250 ml (8½ fl oz/1 cup) thickened (whipping) cream

230 g (8 oz) mild honey dijon mustard

3 tablespoons olive oil

8 French shallots, halved

1.4 kg (3 lb 1 oz) chicken drumsticks

1–2 stems of lemon thyme, leaves picked

SERVES 4

Preheat the oven to 180°C (360°F).

Add the stock, cream and mustard to a bowl. Stir to combine and season with sea salt flakes and freshly ground black pepper. Set aside.

Add the oil to a large high-sided frying pan and place over a medium heat. Once hot, throw in the French shallots and drumsticks. Turn the heat to low and cook for 3–5 minutes or until the chicken looks golden and the shallots are soft, using tongs to turn the chicken and brown on all sides. Add the thyme and cook for another minute or until fragrant.

Scrape all the goodness into a large roasting tin and pour over the stock mixture. Cook in the oven for 30 minutes or until the sauce has thickened and reduced and the chicken is cooked through. Garnish with some extra thyme leaves and serve.

Life goals
TUNA PASTA

Everyone has a version of tuna pasta in their dinner repertoire. This is mine. It's so good eaten in your finest PJs, its immediacy and comfort putting the world at bay. And yet it is so good you also almost want to don a red lip and make a night of it.

It could go either way. Maybe you should let it.

2 tablespoons olive oil

1 onion, diced

3 garlic cloves, crushed

375 ml (12½ fl oz/1½ cups) white wine

800 g (1 lb 12 oz) tinned tomatoes

120 g (4½ oz) smoked kalamata olives, pitted

500 g (1 lb 2 oz) big-arse pasta shells (or pasta of your choice)

500 g (1 lb 2 oz) tinned smoked tuna

finely chopped flat-leaf (Italian) parsley, to serve

SERVES 6

Add the olive oil to a large frying pan and place over a medium heat. Once hot, fry the onion until soft and translucent. Don't rush this step – a lot of the flavour is built here. Add the garlic and cook until fragrant, then add the white wine and simmer for a few minutes before adding the tomatoes and olives. Let her simmer for about 15 minutes more.

Meanwhile, add the pasta to a large pot of ferociously boiling water and cook according to packet instructions or until al dente, then drain.

Add the tuna to the sauce to warm through, giving everything a wee stir before adding the pasta and seasoning with some sea salt flakes and freshly cracked black pepper and topping with the parsley.

SOS

SAVIOURS

With the rush of life, there are far too many things to do, and by the time it gets to dinner, the motivation for 'creating' a meal is between diddly and squat.

There is a time for slow cooking, and prep time, and foraging markets for recipe-specific fresh produce – it's just not today or in this chapter.

These next few pages are for the quick SOS sort of dinners: ones that rely on the kind of simple ingredients that like being in each other's orbit or dishes that rely on a few cupboard staples.

This is for when you need dinner.
And you need it now.

How is it dinnertime again?

PEANUT BUTTER NOODLES

Despite its enthusiastically brief preparation, this is excellent meal-saving fodder. Heavy on the peanut butter, light on your time.

400 g (14 oz) udon noodles

4 tablespoons smooth peanut butter

2 tablespoons Kewpie mayo

1 tablespoon kecap manis

1 teaspoon sesame oil

1 teaspoon Chinese black vinegar

2 tablespoons chicken or vegetable stock

TO SERVE

crunchy chilli oil

finely sliced spring onions (scallions), green part only

fried shallots

SERVES 2–3

Bring a pot of water to the boil. Add the noodles and cook according to packet instructions. While the noodles are cooking, put the remaining ingredients into a bowl and stir to combine. Strain the noodles, return to the pot, add the dressing and, using tongs, gently toss to coat.

Turn out into bowls. Top with some crunchy chilli oil, sliced spring onions and fried shallots. Eat immediately and be bathed in the knowledge that you've survived another day and even sorted something to eat. Sometimes those two things alone are victory enough.

SOS SAVIOURS

Wheels are off

PASTA ALLA VODKA (of sorts)

I refuse to give a quantity for vodka, and I refuse to give a quantity for parmesan. This is a wheels-are-MIA choose your own adventure. Add as life requires.

500 g (1 lb 2 oz) bucatini pasta

1½ cups smoked semi-dried tomatoes (or just semi-dried if that's all you have), plus a few extra, to serve

500 ml (17 fl oz/2 cups) pouring (single) cream

60 ml (2 fl oz/¼ cup) chicken stock

1 tablespoon olive oil

1½ tablespoons tomato paste (concentrated purée)

vodka at will

basil leaves to scatter

parmesan at will, to serve

SERVES 4

Bring a large pot of water to the boil and add the pasta. While the pasta is cooking, put the semi-dried tomatoes, cream and chicken stock in a blender and blitz until combined. This will look weird and clumpy and gross. Ignore it.

Place a large frying pan over a medium heat. Add the olive oil and, once hot, add the tomato paste and cook until it darkens and almost looks like it's separating. Add the clumpy cream mixture and turn down to a simmer. Add the vodka and stir here and there for the remainder of time the pasta is cooking. Taste and add more vodka if required.

When the pasta is ready, use tongs to lift it straight from the pot into the frying pan. You want that little bit of excess pasta water to travel with it for your sauce (and who wants to wash a colander anyway). Cook for 3 minutes, turning the pasta to coat it in the sauce.

Serve into pasta bowls, then top with some basil, as much parmesan as the mood requires and a few extra semi-dried tomatoes. Season generously with a drizzle of olive oil, sea salt flakes and freshly ground black pepper.

Don the stretchy pants. Eat. Order momentarily restored.

Keeping things spicy

SLAB OF SPICY SALMON with A BOWL of SUSHI BITS

Buy salmon from someone you can talk to about your fish. It's an intimate and complicated relationship when it comes to the peach fish. Know where it's coming from. Not all farmed fish is bad, not all wild-caught fish is good – understand the ethics around your fish.

This salmon is intensely flavoured in a good way. It's a hands-off dinner and the perfect cooking method for that very reason. Serve it alongside all the sushi elements.

Cooking on a lower temp is your safety net. You're not going to 'damage' your fish. It's difficult to stuff it up, so if you don't have much confidence cooking fish, this is your ticket.

800 g (1 lb 12 oz) side of salmon

SPICY SAUCE

3 tablespoons crunchy chilli oil

125 g (4½ oz/½ cup) Kewpie mayonnaise

1 tablespoon each rice vinegar, soy sauce, sesame oil and fish sauce

2 garlic cloves, crushed

TO SERVE

steamed rice

1–2 avocados, hulled and sliced

seaweed sheets

furikake

wasabi peas (if they happen to be in the cupboard)

pickled ginger

SERVES 4–6

Preheat the oven to 160°C (320°F).

Combine the spicy sauce ingredients in a bowl. Place the side of salmon, skin side down, on a baking tray lined with baking paper. Smear the sauce generously over the top of the salmon.

Place it in the oven and roast until just cooked through but still medium rare inside, about 12–15 minutes; the flesh will be more translucent, less opaque. If you have salmon that isn't even in thickness, check for doneness in the thickest part of your fish.

Remove from the oven and transfer to a serving dish. Serve with all the sushi bits alongside – rice, avo, seaweed, a sprinkle of furikake and wasabi peas if you happen to have them.

Serve it.

Another dinner done.

A TIN OF TOONS and GREEN THINGS MAKETH A MEAL

The places a tin of toooona can take you are many and plentiful. This humble stuff can make a glorious meal in moments – its place in your cupboard stores should never be underestimated. Just make it tuna in olive oil; the tuna in water tastes of atrocity, and you owe the tuna so much more than that. Bonus points if your toons are smoked.

If grilling lettuce is a step too far and makes you feel like you are farming silkworms, you can omit this step entirely, but the contrast between the crisp, cool centres and caramelised exterior is proof that opposites attract.

4 baby cos (romaine) lettuces, halved

olive oil for brushing

325 g (11½ oz) tinned smoked tuna

fresh herbs and crusty bread, to serve

HERBY CASHEW DRESSING

155 g (5½ oz/1 cup) cashews

½ cup basil leaves

juice and zest of ½ large lemon (about 2 tablespoons juice)

1 heaped tablespoon honey

salt and pepper, to season

fresh herbs, to serve

SERVES 2–3

Place a chargrill pan over a medium heat. Brush the baby cos with the olive oil like a nineties woman with a bottle of Le Tan at the beach – liberal and plentiful helps get this the colour it needs. Grill cut side down until charred (2–3 minutes). Turn and grill other side (2–3 minutes), then chuck it on a large serving dish.

While your lettuce is working on its tan, add all the herby cashew dressing ingredients to a blender along with 125 ml (4 fl oz/½ cup) water, season with salt and pepper, and blitz until you have a smoooooooth consistency. It might need a few turns through the blender. If you hate any hint of sweet in your dressing, just ditch the honey entirely here.

Place lettuce on a serving plate.

Strain the tuna from its oil and scoop onto the lettuce, then drizzle over the dressing. Season with sea salt flakes and freshly ground black pepper or a squeeze of lemon juice. Throw some herbs in at the last minute if you feel fancy and serve immediately with some crusty bread.

HOT TIP This dressing is good on all manner of crisp leaves. You can also smear it across a piece of piping hot grilled salmon for a last-minute but very respectable juju for dinner.

A few eggs and a whim

A COUPLE of EGGS

If you have eggs, you have a meal.

SESAME FRIED EGGS

PER SERVE

1 tablespoon olive oil

1 tablespoon white sesame seeds

1 egg

pinch of Turkish red pepper flakes

a few saffron threads (if you happen to have them)

toast or steamed rice, to serve

pinch of chopped flat-leaf (Italian) parsley, to serve

SERVES 1

Put the oil in a frying pan and place over a medium heat. Add the sesame seeds and swirl the pan until they begin to colour. Turn heat to high and carefully break the egg into the pan. Scoop some seeds onto the egg white as it starts to colour and add the chilli flakes and saffron if you have it. Cook to your liking. Serve on toast or rice and season with sea salt flakes, freshly ground black pepper and chopped parsley.

CHEESE 'n' PEPPER EGGS EN COCOTTE

PER SERVE

2 eggs

2 tablespoons pouring (single) cream

1 tablespoon grated parmesan

1 tablespoon grated pecorino

SERVES 1

Combine one of the eggs, the cream and the cheeses in a bowl. Pour into an individual frying pan and place over a medium heat. Cook for 1–2 minutes or until the surface looks firm and the edges start to puff and brown. Crack the second egg on top and cook for another minute or two. You can speed this up by popping under the grill (broiler) for 1 minute to cook to your liking. Season with sea salt flakes and a lot of freshly ground black pepper.

SAUCY BAKED EGGS

400–500 g (14 oz–1 lb 2 oz) jarred pasta sauce (arrabbiata works a treat)

a few basil leaves, plus extra to serve

¼ cup chopped olives

6–8 eggs

175 g (6 oz) mozzarella, broken into chunks

fresh sourdough, to serve

SERVES 3–4

Preheat the oven to 180°C (360°F).

Pour the sauce into a large ovenproof dish. Tear over the basil leaves. Scatter over the olives and season with some salt and ground black pepper. Using a spoon, make slight indents in the sauce and crack an egg into each divot. Scatter the mozzarella chunks and pop in the oven until cooked to your liking, about 10–12 minutes for a medium–soft yolk. Scatter over more basil and season well with salt and ground black pepper. Serve with some hunks of sourdough.

TO MAKE THIS EXTRA Add chilli flakes, fried capers and anchovies.

BAKED BAGEL EGGS

half a bagel

pinch each of curry powder, ground cumin, garam masala, brown mustard seeds and ground turmeric

2 tablespoons soft salted butter

1–2 eggs

fried curry leaves, to serve

SERVES 1

Preheat the oven to 180°C (360°F).

Use a cookie cutter to widen the centre hole of the bagel half. Combine the spices with the butter in a bowl and spread over the cut side of the bagel, reserving a dollop for the eggs. Put the bagel on a baking tray lined with baking paper. Crack 1–2 eggs into the hole and put the extra dollop of butter on top. Bake in the oven to your liking, about 10 minutes for a soft yolk. Top with fried curry leaves.

Orbs of goodness

CARAMELISED ONION and HARISSA CHICKPEAS with CORIANDER DRIZZLY STUFF

Chickpeas – the ultimate player. Happy to get down 'n' dirty with hefty proteins or a mass of green vegetation. It judges none and beds them all.

Here the tryst belongs squarely with some long-cooked onions and harissa, with a yoghurt finisher. You'll want seconds.

3 tablespoons olive oil, plus extra to drizzle

2 large onions, finely sliced

6 garlic cloves

2–3 tablespoons harissa paste, plus extra to drizzle

2 × 425 g (15 oz) tins chickpeas, drained and rinsed

250 ml (8½ oz/1 cup) coconut milk

yoghurt, to serve

½ cup finely chopped coriander (cilantro) leaves, to serve

SERVES 4 WITH RICE AND/OR NAAN

Place a frying pan over a medium–low heat. Add the oil and, once hot, fry the onions for 10 minutes or until completely soft and translucent, stirring often. Add the garlic and harissa paste and cook until the onion is coated in the mixture and has darkened in colour, 1–2 minutes, stirring regularly. Add the chickpeas and coconut milk and turn the heat to low. Stir gently while it simmers until the chickpeas warm through and the mixture has reduced slightly. Season with sea salt flakes and freshly ground black pepper.

Turn the chickpeas into serving bowls and top with a dollop of yoghurt. Combine the extra olive oil and harissa paste and drizzle over the top of the yoghurt. Finish with the chopped coriander and serve.

GO LARGE Scatter with chopped smoked almonds and even some dried rose petals.

BUT I DON'T HAVE ... No coconut milk? It's an easy sub with yoghurt.

Life in freefall

CHICKEN and COUSCOUS BAKE

If a dish could hold your hand, quietly, calmly, full of love and kindness, this is it. Throw it in. Give it a toss, shove it in the oven and then, with the glorious alchemy of cooking, out comes dinner.

Proof that your cooking is a vessel of care for others.

1 kg (2 lb 3 oz) chicken thighs, cut into bite-sized chunks

250 g (9 oz) pearl couscous

60 ml (2 fl oz/¼ cup) olive oil

1 teaspoon each salt flakes, ground turmeric, ground cumin and sumac

3 garlic cloves, crushed

2 tablespoons tomato paste (concentrated purée)

1 tablespoon pomegranate syrup or date syrup or honey

625 ml (21 fl oz/2½ cups) boiling chicken stock

TO SERVE

chopped coriander (cilantro) and parsley leaves

smoked almonds

fried onions

QUICK LEMON SUMAC DRESSING (OPTIONAL)

juice of 1 lemon

½ cup Greek yoghurt

sumac to taste

SERVES 4-6

Preheat the oven to 180°C (360°F).

Put the chicken and couscous in a roasting tin. Drizzle over the olive oil. Add the spices, garlic, tomato paste and syrup, giving it all a quick toss to combine, then spread out evenly.

Pour over the chicken stock, place a piece of baking paper on top to touch and then wrap tightly with foil. Shove in the oven for 30 minutes.

After 30 minutes, remove the foil and baking paper and return to the oven for another 15 minutes or until the liquid has been absorbed and the chicken is cooked through.

If making the dressing, quickly combine the ingredients in a bowl.

Garnish with the dressing (if using), chopped coriander and parsley, smoked almonds and fried onions.

EATING-
OUT-LOUD

LIP-
SMACKERS

I wish I could only eat lip-smackers. Meals that surprise and delight. A wham of spice, nose-clearing heat or an unexpected flavour pairing that makes one thing taste like something entirely indescribable. I live for these little hits – we need them. The drudgery of a Wednesday night is vastly improved by the kind of food that makes your mouth come alive, your spine tingle just a touch. The kind of superlative surprise that makes every other meal (meat and three veg, I am looking at you) seem like unnecessary decoration and polishing.

These are by no means complicated or fancy. But they are the sort of dishes that get in your face. Intimately. They never would have survived social distancing, and thank goodness for that.

Not your meat and three veg

MINUTE STEAK
with
ROASTED THAI
TOMATOES

Remember when you were little and how a visit from your cool aunt made you feel? You know the one: she smelled like wine breath and was full of inappropriate conversation, and you just freaking loved every second of it. This is that feeling in a dinner. All spice and delight and surprise mixed with midweek convenience.

2 tablespoons brown sugar

juice and zest of 1 large lime

1½ tablespoons Thai red curry paste

850 g (1 lb 14 oz) cherry tomatoes

800 g (1 lb 12 oz) rump steaks

1–2 tablespoons olive oil

Thai basil leaves, to serve

2 makrut lime leaves, veins removed and finely sliced, to serve

SERVES 4–6

Preheat the oven to 180°C (360°F).

Combine the sugar, lime juice and zest and curry paste in a bowl. If it doesn't seem like much, add additional lime juice and sugar – you want enough to lightly coat your tomatoes. Spread the tomatoes across a roasting tin and pour over the curry paste mixture, tossing gently to combine. Roast in the oven for 30 minutes.

When the tomatoes have 10 minutes remaining, preheat a lightly greased chargrill pan over a high heat or a barbecue hotplate. Brush steaks with oil and season with salt and ground black pepper. Cook, turning occasionally, until well browned (5–6 minutes). Set aside to rest for 5 minutes.

To serve, cut your steak into thick slices. Spoon the tomatoes and all the juicy caramelised bits onto plates and top with the sliced steak. Top with Thai basil leaves and sliced makrut lime leaves. Season with salt and serve.

Dinnertime nirvana
KUNG PAO CAULIFLOWER

Proof that your dinner doesn't need a pulse. I happily eat this one on repeat. Such a treasured favourite with all the childhood takeout feels.

1 small head of cauliflower cut into florets

flavourless oil to coat

4 dried red chillies, halved lengthways, seeds removed

KUNG PAO SAUCE

120 ml (4 fl oz) each hoisin sauce, sweet soy sauce and Chinese black vinegar

2 tablespoons each sesame oil, oyster sauce, soy sauce and brown sugar

1 teaspoon ground sichuan pepper (substitute ground white pepper corns if unavailable)

4 garlic cloves, finely grated

1½ tablespoons freshly grated ginger

4 teaspoons cornflour (cornstarch)

TO SERVE

1 generous handful spring onions (scallions), sliced

80–120 g (2¾–4½ oz/½–¾ cup) salted peanuts

fried shallots

steamed jasmine or coconut rice

SERVES 4 WITH RICE

Preheat the oven to 215°C (420°F).

Place the cauliflower florets in a non-stick roasting tin, drizzle with enough oil to very lightly coat and season generously with salt. Roast for 15–18 minutes – you want them to be slightly crisp and having a few gnarly tanned bits.

While the cauliflower is roasting, whisk all the kung pao sauce ingredients together in a bowl until combined. You may need to whisk a few times to eliminate any lumps and bumps of cornflour.

Pull the cauliflower from the oven and pour the sauce all over, add the dried chillies and use tongs to turn and coat the cauliflower pieces in the sauce. Return the roasting tin to the oven.

Roast for another 15 minutes, stirring and tossing the cauliflower a few times during cooking to prevent burning. Remove and scatter with the spring onions, peanuts and fried shallots and serve with rice. You could also add some sliced fresh red chilli for extra colour and heat.

Holy hell this is good

SPICY SICHUAN TOMATO SHALLOT

3 French shallots, finely diced

2 tablespoons finely grated fresh ginger

4 lemongrass stems, white part only, finely chopped

6 garlic cloves, finely chopped

2 tablespoons olive oil

40 g (1½ oz) salted butter

140 g (5 oz) tomato paste (concentrated purée)

1 tablespoon crushed sichuan peppercorns

3 tablespoons soy sauce

2 tablespoons hoisin sauce

2 tablespoons caster (superfine) sugar

1½ tablespoons nutritional yeast flakes

700 g (1 lb 9 oz) dried pulled noodles

½ cup finely chopped coriander (cilantro) leaves

200 g (7 oz/2 cups) parmesan, finely grated

SAUCY GOODNESS FINISHER

2 tablespoons mixed toasted sesame seeds

2 tablespoons fried shallots

80 ml (2½ fl oz/⅓ cup) sesame oil

1 tablespoon crushed sichuan peppercorns

juice of 1 lime

**SERVES 4
(OR 5 RESTRAINED EATERS)**

Lip-smacking, spine-tingling deliciousness. If I could reach through the pages and shake you gently by the shoulders, in a non-threatening way but one that gets my point across (*you need to make this STAT*), I absolutely would.

There is a little bit of chopping frippery, but it's momentary, and the rest of this comes together quickly and tastes like all the good things in life squeezed into a bowl. I use the dried pulled noodles you can get from Costco. It's no-frills, buy-the-big-arse-box excellence. Highly recommend.

BUTTER NOODLES

To make the saucy goodness finisher, whisk all the ingredients in a small bowl until combined. Set aside.

Combine the shallots, ginger, lemongrass and garlic in a bowl. Place a frying pan over a medium–low heat. Add the olive oil and, once hot, fry the combined aromatics for 2–3 minutes or until softening and fragrant. Add the butter and continue to cook until the butter is bubbling but not taking on any colour. Add the tomato paste and cook until the paste darkens and is fully incorporated in the butter mixture, then add the sichuan peppercorns, soy sauce, hoisin, sugar and yeast flakes. Turn to a very low simmer while you bring a pot of water to the boil.

Cook your noodles according to the packet instructions. When you are a minute shy of the cooking time, fish the noodles out using a pair of tongs and add directly to the glorious sauce mixture. Add in a ladle or two of the cooking water to help loosen the sauce and, using tongs, turn the noodles so they are well-coated.

Add the coriander and the parmesan, reserving a sprinkle, and continue cooking. Add more cooking water if you feel it's not coating the noodles enough.

To serve, sprinkle over the reserved parmesan for good measure and then spoon over your saucy goodness finisher. Eat with an old shirt on and your hair tied back so you can lean over and really get involved with your meal – it's the only way.

Winner, winner, bean dinner

BROTHY BUTTER BEANS with SPINACH and CHERMOULA

2 tablespoons olive oil

1 French shallot, halved and finely sliced

90 g (3 oz/⅓ cup) tomato paste (concentrated purée)

310 ml (10½ fl oz/1¼ cups) chicken or vegetable stock

2 × 400 g (14 oz) tins butter beans, drained and rinsed

2–3 generous handfuls baby spinach

hunk of Persian feta, to serve

QUICK CHERMOULA

1 tablespoon each ground cumin and ground coriander

juice and zest of 2 lemons

1½ cups mixed herbs (I use coriander/cilantro and flat-leaf/Italian parsley)

250 ml (8½ fl oz/1 cup) olive oil

4 garlic cloves

2 teaspoons each sumac, aleppo pepper and sweet smoked paprika

1 heaped teaspoon ground turmeric

2 teaspoons caster (superfine) sugar

very generous pinch of sea salt flakes

SERVES 4 (JUST) WITH A HUNK OF BREAD FOR MOPPING

This is a big bowl of wet and it's excellent. Swimming beans should be part of everyone's week.

This is not the meal to serve with your best cutlery as you lightly discuss current affairs and pretentiously swirl a glass of pet nat. This is more the hunker-down-with-slabs-of-bread-for-mopping kind of meal. It's quick, it's damn delicious and, best of all, it's so very comforting.

Also, you could blitz the whole lot in a blender at the end and call it soup – heck, you could pop into a geriatric ward with the leftovers. Look at you go, angel.

I acknowledge busy, so you could use store-bought chermoula rather than making your own, or swap it out for harissa – just watch the heat.

Add the quick chermoula ingredients to a food processor and blitz to combine. Set aside.

Pop a frying pan over a medium heat and, once hot, add the oil. Fry the French shallot until soft, then add in 2–3 tablespoons of the chermoula. Give it a stir until fragrant then add the tomato paste. Cook until the paste has darkened and looks like it is coming away from the pan. Pour in the stock and add the beans, then simmer on low until the beans are warmed through. If it doesn't seem quite saucy enough, add a little more stock.

Remove from the heat. You can stir the spinach leaves through here or pour the beans into bowls already laden with spinach. Top with a spoonful of Persian feta then spoon over a tablespoon or two of the chermoula. Season with sea salt flakes and freshly ground black pepper and serve.

Curry night delight

FISH CURRY, HEAVY

Curry night done right.

This is not the kind of curry heat that causes you to momentarily pass out then come to, numb from nipple to knee. No, this is subtle, fragrant and delightful rather than confronting. A curry that understands the brutalities of a long and busy week.

on the LEMONGRASS

3 tablespoons coconut oil

400 ml (13½ fl oz) coconut cream

60 ml (2 fl oz/¼ cup) fish stock

fish sauce, lime juice and sugar, to season

300–400 g (10½–14 oz) white fish cut into large chunks the size of a matchbox

PASTE

2 French shallots, chopped

6 garlic cloves, chopped

3 lemongrass stems, pale part only, finely sliced

2 makrut lime leaves, deveined and chopped

2 heaped tablespoons finely grated fresh ginger

1 teaspoon each ground cumin and ground coriander

1 heaped cup coriander leaves

1 tablespoon oyster sauce

1 tablespoon caster (superfine) sugar

juice and zest of 1 lime

1 green chilli or jalapeño, seeds removed (optional)

TO SERVE

steamed rice

1–2 cups roughly chopped greens, such broccolini or green beans

sliced spring onions (scallions)

½ cup Asian herbs

fried shallots

lime wedges

SERVES 4

Combine the paste ingredients in a small food processor. Blitz to a paste-like consistency.

Add the oil to a frying pan over a medium heat. Once hot, fry the paste until fragrant, stirring constantly to prevent catching and for no more than 1 minute. Add the coconut cream and stock and simmer until slightly reduced. Taste and check for seasoning – you can correct it with fish sauce, lime juice and sugar. You want a balance of sweet, salty and then that lovely fragrant hit of aromatics.

Add the pieces of fish and turn the heat down to a simmer. Let them poach for 4–5 minutes or until just cooked through.

Season again then spoon the curry over bowls of rice. I like to add the greens raw and push them into the hot curry so they are warm but still have all their freshness and crunch. Top generously with the spring onions, coriander and fried shallots. Give everything a good squeeze of lime juice and serve.

Spine-tingling can't-get-enough-of-it lip-smacker

CRUNCHY STUFF with CHICKEN SALAD

Look, this road is as high as it is low. You'll be in the noodle aisle, university-student style buying up 2-minute noodles as much as you'll be in the deli aisle throwing posh packets of crisps into your basket with wild abandon. But both experiences turn this into one of the best things you will put in your mouth. Ever.

1 small rotisserie chicken, meat roughly shredded

100 g (3½ oz/⅔ cup) fresh peas

90 g (3 oz/1 cup) bean sprouts

1 cup sugar-snap peas

3–4 radishes, finely sliced

½ telegraph (long) cucumber, cut into matchsticks

leaves of 1 bunch coriander

leaves of 1 bunch mint

DRESSING

125 ml (4 fl oz/½ cup) coconut milk

2 tablespoons sweet chilli sauce

1 tablespoon brown sugar

1 tablespoon fish sauce

1 tablespoon lime juice

CRUNCH

2–3 packets 2-minute noodles

¼ cup olive oil

40 g (1½ oz) prawn crackers

40 g (1½ oz) pork scratchings

40 g (1½ oz) burger rings

½ cup fried shallots

SERVES 4–6

Preheat the oven to 180°C (360°F).

To make the crunch, roughly break up the 2-minute noodles and spread across a baking tray. Drizzle with the olive oil and scatter over the packet of seasoning. Pop in the oven and cook for 20 minutes or until the noodles have taken on a golden colour. Once cooled add to a large zip lock bag with the remaining ingredients and seal. Gently give it a few taps with a rolling pin to break up the large crisps. You don't want a fine crumb, you want chunks and crisp and interest.

Make the dressing by adding all ingredients to a bowl and whisking to combine.

Add all the salad ingredients to a large bowl and, using your hands, toss to combine. Drizzle over some dressing – you want this to only just coat the salad, so there may be some left over.

Place on a serving platter and spoon over the crunchy mix generously just before serving.

OYSTER MUSHROOM SHAWARMA

I love serving these heaped on a plate for people to build pitas for themselves, but if share plates aren't for you, skewer the mushrooms following the quick pan-fry, then pop in the oven to finish cooking.

You can do the whole lot in the frying pan and skip the oven component, but it's difficult to manage the heat and you don't want to burn the spices. Watch carefully. I like to sear them in the pan like you would any protein and finish them off a little more gently in the oven.

500 g (1 lb 2 oz) oyster mushrooms

80 ml (2½ fl oz/⅓ cup) olive oil

3 tablespoons salted butter

SPICE MIX

1 tablespoon each ground cumin and ground coriander

1 teaspoon each ground allspice, sweet paprika, ground turmeric, ground black pepper and onion powder

½ teaspoon each cayenne pepper, ground cardamom and ground cinnamon

generous pinch of brown sugar

TO SERVE

hummus

garlic yoghurt sauce

flatbreads or pitas

coriander (cilantro) and mint leaves

SERVES 4–6

Preheat the oven to 200°C (390°F). Line a roasting tin with baking paper.

For the spice mix, combine all the ingredients in a small bowl.

In another bowl, mix the mushrooms with half the spice mix. Add 2 tablespoons of the olive oil and toss very gently to coat the mushrooms in the mixture.

Add the remaining oil and the butter to a frying pan and place over a medium heat. Add a few of the mushrooms, being careful not to overcrowd your pan, and cook for 2 minutes or until they're taking on some colour. Transfer to your roasting tin and repeat with the remaining mushrooms. Sprinkle over the rest of the spice mix and toss gently with tongs to coat. Drizzle over a little more olive oil if needed and finish in the oven for 15–20 minutes, turning a few times during cooking.

Serve with hummus, garlic yoghurt sauce, flatbreads or pitas, and fresh coriander and mint.

Also amazing if you stuff some piping hot fries in a pita with the mushrooms … just an afterthought, but a good one.

The alchemy of slow cooking
HERBY LAMB and DATE SLOW-COOKED GOODNESS

I love the surprise of this. Based on khoresh-e ghormeh sabzi (a Persian herb, bean and lamb stew), it's an ode to herbs – everything else is the second act. I've added dates to help thicken the sauce and add a beautifully subtle sweetness and richness.

Hint hint: double batch it.

Traditionally, Persian black limes are added for a beautiful yet subtle sour element. These can be a little tricky to come by, so for convenience you can substitute with extra sumac. Do try to find the limes though – they add a sublime element to this low 'n' slow number.

---

1 kg (2 lb 3 oz) butterflied lamb leg, chopped into large bite-sized pieces

1 tablespoon ground turmeric

1 teaspoon sumac, plus extra to serve

4 garlic cloves, finely chopped

3 tablespoons olive oil

2 teaspoons dried fenugreek seeds

2 onions, diced

1 litre (34 fl oz/4 cups) chicken stock

180 g (6½ oz/1 cup) pitted dates, chopped

1 dried Persian black lime (or substitute an additional teaspoon of sumac)

lemon juice, to serve

HERB MIXTURE

leaves from 2 large bunches flat-leaf (Italian) parsley

leaves from 2 large bunches coriander (cilantro)

1 large bunch chives

1 bunch spring onions (scallions)

3 tablespoons olive oil

SERVES 4–6

Add the chopped lamb, turmeric, sumac, garlic, olive oil and fenugreek to a bowl and toss to combine.

Place a stockpot or very large saucepan over a medium heat. Once hot, add the lamb and brown all over for 5–10 minutes. It's important not to rush this step – you want the meat to brown and the fat to caramelise.

Push the lamb to the side and add the onion, stirring to prevent catching, until softened, about another 5 minutes.

Add 750 ml (25½ fl oz/3 cups) of the stock and bring to a boil. Reduce to a low heat and add the dates and the Persian lime. With the lid partially on the pot, simmer for about 1½ hours (or up to 3 hours). You want the meat to break apart with a fork and the liquid to have mostly reduced.
I always like to have the spare cup of stock in case the liquid evaporates before the cooking time is up, so add from that if it's beginning to look too dry.

For the herb mixture, pulse the parsley and coriander leaves in a food processor until very finely chopped, then transfer to a bowl. Chop the chives and spring onions by hand as finely as possible and add to the herbs. (You can't chop these in the food processor as they will just turn to mush.) Put the 3 tablespoons of oil in a frying pan over a medium heat. Add the herb mixture and cook for 10 minutes, stirring constantly to prevent burning, until they become quite dry. It seems a little counterintuitive to cook fresh herbs like this but it is where so much of the stew's flavour comes from. Stir the herb mixture into the lamb towards the end of its cooking time and simmer for about 20 minutes.

Squeeze over some lemon juice and season with salt, freshly ground black pepper and more sumac to taste just prior to serving. Serve as is or with steamed rice.

Pie for your pie hole

MASALA CHICKEN 'n' POTATO POT PIE for a (small) CROWD

Controversial, I know, but I've used ancho chilli powder in this recipe – I love the more subtle smoky flavour. Mexican chillies in an Indian-inspired dish might seem confusing, but they give a generous, rounded warmth rather than a sheen of forehead sweat. It's gentle, an introduction to curry, if you will. It also means I could feed this pie to a baby.

This makes about 2½ cups of paste, so you can freeze the other half for another curry in a hurry. Ditto if you double batched the sauce, so you could pull a pie in minutes.

2 tablespoons ghee

1.2 kg (2 lb 10 oz) whole chicken thighs

2 × 400 ml (13½ fl oz) tins coconut milk

600 g (1 lb 5 oz/4 cups) small white potatoes, diced

1 × 375 g (13 oz) sheet butter puff pastry

1 egg

2 tablespoons milk

MASALA PASTE

2 onions, chopped

8 garlic cloves, chopped

2 heaped tablespoons finely grated fresh ginger

⅓ cup garam masala

½ tablespoon sea salt flakes

2 tablespoons ancho chilli powder

1 teaspoon caster (superfine) sugar

1 teaspoon each fenugreek seeds and ground cloves

1 tablespoon each ground coriander, ground turmeric and ground cumin

juice and zest of 2 limes

1 handful coriander (cilantro) leaves, chopped

115 g (4 oz/¾ cup) toasted cashews

2 tablespoons tomato paste (concentrated purée)

SERVES 8

Put the masala paste ingredients in a food processor and blitz to a coarse paste.

Add the ghee to a frying pan over a medium heat. Once hot, add half the paste, about 1 cup, and cook until fragrant and the paste looks like it is going to split. Add the chicken and cook until lightly browned all over. Add the coconut milk and give everything a good stir, then turn the heat down to a moderately active simmer. This is a sauce on a health kick: it's sweating and bubbling a little with the effort but can't quite go for a run yet.

After about 30 minutes, stir in the potatoes then simmer for another 30 minutes. You want to ensure some evaporation has occurred so you don't have a soupy pie. Preheat the oven to 180°C (360°F).

Pour the mixture into a roasting tin approximately 32 × 24 × 5 cm (12½ × 9½ × 2 in) and lay the sheet of puff pastry over the top. Gently press down along all the edges, or tuck in around the filling like you might put a blanket over a small child. Using a fork, lightly prick the pastry all over the surface. Briefly whisk the egg and milk in a small bowl. Brush the pie with the egg wash and pop in the oven for 45 minutes.

Serve piping hot. With pie, it's the only way.

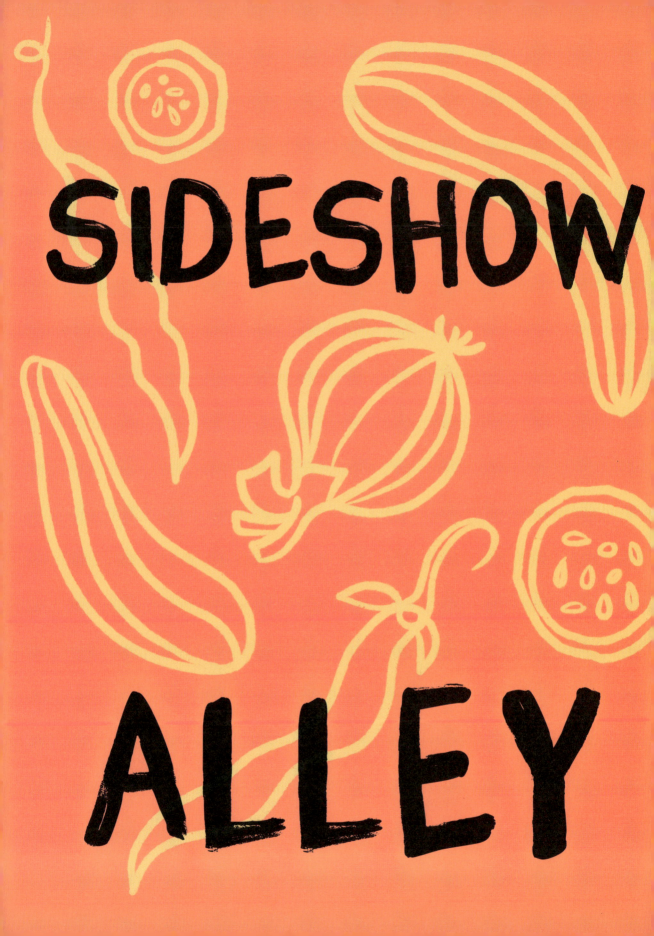

Sides maketh the meal. They are the greatest wonders of mealtime or the worst, depending on how you organise your breathing.

A good side will improve the simplest of proteins. Like a polite guest, it brings the texture, the vibrancy, the colour and the fun. You can't fault it.

Good sides make me want to eat as much as possible as soon as possible. A steak is always going to be just a steak. Yes, the quality of the cooking and flavour (fat) of the meat will vary, but it's the sides served alongside that push it into a new territory entirely.

A good side dish should induce the rare but highly applicable Stendhal syndrome. This aesthetic condition is brought on by beauty (in this case, the side) and causes intense and dramatic crowd-gathering physical responses like fainting, the sweats and chest pain.

While I wouldn't like you to pass out, I do want you to enjoy some of my favourite sides, designed to maximise enjoyment and your Thursday night dinner. Some with flavours that will smack you around the chops a little, some with butter, and some so tasty you'll just want to get in there and eat with your hands.

SLOW-ROASTED CABBAGE with MADRAS CURRY BUTTER

Inexpensive and infinitely versatile with an impressively long shelf life, one head of cabbage goes a long way, and this dish is a keeper. People rave. And it is literally cabbage and a bit of spiced butter – a low-effort, high-reward dish that has you quietly fist-pumping your success behind the pantry door.

It's a long hands-off cook, so plan accordingly.

1 head of cabbage, trimmed, cut into quarters

olive oil to drizzle

125 g (4½ oz) salted butter (or more to taste)

1 tablespoon madras curry powder (or to taste)

SERVES 6 AS PART OF A SPREAD

Preheat the oven to 160°C (320°F) and line a roasting tin with baking paper. Place the cabbage pieces in the tin and drizzle with a little olive oil. Roast until caramelised and tender and a skewer can be inserted with little resistance (4½–5 hours).

Place a saucepan over a medium heat. Add the butter and, once foaming, add the curry powder. Give it a few swirls then immediately remove from the heat – you don't want to burn the curry powder.

Gently transfer the cabbage to a serving plate. Pour the butter over slowly so it has time to seep and ooze inappropriately into the layers of cabbage.

Season with salt and serve immediately.

If you happen to have a smoker, you want to smoke your cabbage for 4 hours at about 170°C (340°F). Then follow the recipe from melting the butter onwards.

Can't get your hands on madras curry powder? Simply substitute with your cupboard staple of Keen's.

SIDESHOW ALLEY

The essence of summer

LIME-MARINATED CUKES with WHIPPED CASHEW SAMBAL

I objected to eating the discharge of tortured nuts for some time, but what a fool's game that was – it is pure creamy glory. Here the sambal-whipped cashews are the perfect base for some lime-hit cucumbers. I'd eat this as a snack or served alongside any grilled proteins for a little something extra.

You can make the whipped goodness ahead of time and pop in the fridge. Bring to room temp before serving, and if still too firm you can loosen it with a tablespoon or two of water.

155 g (5½ oz/1 cup) cashew nuts

1 small garlic clove, chopped

1½ tablespoons finely grated fresh ginger

1 tablespoon each soy sauce, sweet soy sauce and sambal oelek

1 tablespoon honey

4 limes

2 long (telegraph) cucumbers

6 finely sliced mint leaves, to serve

SERVES 4 AS A SIDE (OBVS)

To make the cashew sambal, bring a pot of water to the boil. Remove from the heat, add the cashews and set aside for at least 30 minutes (or up to 2 hours or overnight in the fridge) to soften. Drain then put the cashew nuts along with the garlic, ginger, sauces, honey and the juice and zest of two of the limes in a blender. Pulse until a smooth and creamy dip-like consistency is achieved.

Thickly slice your cucumbers and pop in a bowl. Mix through the juice and zest of the two remaining limes and set aside for 15 minutes.

To serve, scoop the cashew sambal onto a plate. Top with the lime-addled cukes and the finely sliced mint leaves.

You need to eat these on repeat

SLOW-COOKED PUTTANESCA ONIONS

80 ml (2½ fl oz/⅓ cup) olive oil

4 garlic cloves, chopped

6 anchovies in oil

large pinch of Turkish red pepper flakes or dried chilli flakes (but adjust according to heat preference)

140 g (5 oz) tomato paste (concentrated purée)

1 kg (2 lb 3 oz) baby onions, halved

2 tablespoons capers in brine plus 2 tablespoons of the brining liquid

30 g (1 oz/¼ cup) pitted black olives, chopped

125 ml (4 fl oz/½ cup) tomato passata (puréed tomatoes)

1 tablespoon caster (superfine) sugar

SERVES 4-6

I love the mythology surrounding how this classic came into being. Puttanesca literally translates to 'in the style of prostitutes' supposedly because the pungent aromas of garlic, anchovies, capers and olives tossed with pasta were how Neapolitan sex workers would lead customers to their doors. Whatever the origins, what does well slipping between strands of pasta does equally well sliding down some onions.

This recipe epitomises the concept of doing a lot with a little, and I am also revealing a bias: my love for slow-cooked onions shows no signs of slowing down. They are always cheap, and with a little tender loving care they can be transformed into something else entirely. Gratification without complication.

I strongly suggest serving these with something meaty adjacent. They are also great smeared across a piece of toast and washed down with an icy chardy or superbly made G&T.

Preheat the oven to 160°C (320°F).

Heat the oil in a 24 cm (9½ in) ovenproof frying pan over a low heat. Once hot, fry the garlic and anchovy fillets, stirring to prevent the garlic taking on too much colour, until the anchovies have melted into the oil. Add the red pepper or chilli flakes and tomato paste and cook until the paste comes away from the pan and darkens in colour.

Push the onion halves into the tomato paste mixture. Add the capers, brining liquid and olives. Give everything a little push around so it's snug in the pan. Pour over the passata and sprinkle with the sugar.

Pop the pan into the oven and cook for 45 minutes up to 1½ hours or until the onions are caramelised and golden (a bit of char here and there is also excellent) and the sauce looks sticky and mostly reduced.

Season with sea salt flakes and freshly ground black pepper and serve.

HOT TIP You can throw the lot in a blender with a splash of water and a little more passata for a pasta sauce of the gods. Throw a tin of tuna on top. Eat. Repeat.

Tomatoes for the soul

PASTRAMI- SPICED TOMS with PICKLED YOGHURT

I use a combo of yoghurt (for the tang) and crème fraiche (for that velvety mouthfeel), but I am a hedonist, so go forth and use just a cup of yoghurt if that is what you have on hand.

2 tablespoons pastrami seasoning

2 tablespoons soft brown sugar

60 ml (2 fl oz/¼ cup) olive oil, plus extra for roasting

1 kg (2 lb 3 oz) cherry tomatoes on the vine

125 ml (4 fl oz/½ cup) yoghurt

125 ml (4 fl oz/½ cup) crème fraiche

2 tablespoons finely diced pickles, plus 2 tablespoons liquid from the jar

SERVES 4-6 AS PART OF A MEAL

Preheat the oven to 150°C (300°F).

Combine the pastrami seasoning, sugar and olive oil in a bowl. Add the tomatoes and use your hands to rub over the mixture. Spread the tomatoes across a large roasting tin, scraping out every bit of mixture with them. Give them an extra lug of olive oil then roast for 45 minutes or until your house smells warm, spicy and a little bit like a pizza shop.

About 10 minutes from serving, combine the yoghurt, crème fraiche, pickles and pickling liquid in a bowl. Season generously with sea salt flakes and freshly ground black pepper. If this seems a bit runny, pop it in the fridge to firm up a little or just add another dollop of yoghurt.

Smear the yoghurt mixture over a serving platter. Top with the pastrami-seasoned roast tomatoes. Spoon over any cooking liquids and serve to accolades.

HOT TIP To make your own pastrami seasoning, combine 1 tablespoon each of freshly ground black pepper, coriander powder, brown sugar and sweet smoked paprika in a bowl along with 2 teaspoons each of garlic powder, onion powder and mild yellow mustard powder.

Holy sh*t yum!

BLACK
PEPPER
BEANS

These are a total mouth party. I can't stop eating them. This is not just a plate of beans. Over a bowl of coconut rice, I think these could easily move into dinner rather than side territory.

It's a 10-minute win. And we all need those.

2 tablespoons grapeseed or other flavourless oil

4 heaped cups green beans, topped and tailed

100 ml (3½ fl oz) each kecap manis and soy sauce

2 makrut lime leaves, deveined and finely sliced, to serve

BLACK PEPPER PASTE

1 tablespoon grapeseed oil

⅓ cup coarsely grated ginger

3 garlic cloves, roughly chopped

3 French shallots, roughly chopped

3 tablespoons black peppercorns, lightly crushed in a mortar and pestle

4–6 makrut lime leaves, deveined and roughly chopped

SERVES 4–6

For the black pepper paste, put all the ingredients into a blender and process to a coarse paste.

Place a frying pan over a high heat until smoking. Add the oil and, when hot, fry the paste until fragrant. Add the beans and continue frying, turning regularly so they become coated in the paste (maximum 1 minute). Add the sweet soy and soy sauce and cook until the beans are coated in the sauce.

Remove the beans to a serving plate and let the sauce cook down for another minute – you want it all to be a bit caramelised and gnarly. Spoon the reduced goodness over the beans, top with the sliced makrut lime leaves and serve.

Roasted veg glow-up
CHARRED BROCCOLINI with BROWN BUTTER MAYO, PARTY CRUNCH and a FEW GOLDEN RAISINS

The brown butter mayo combo with warm, charred, sweet broc, and then the one-two punch of the party crunch. This is living, people. This. Is. Living.

Mayo is one of the cheapest condiments you can make. And this version, heavy on the butter instead of oil, is a glorious game changer and perfect bedfellow for roasted veg. There is something about giving the arms a workout with some old-fashioned whisk labour that just makes this so much more reliable. I also recommend the old-school way because you are emulsifying butter, not oil, and it responds a little differently.

2 heads of broccoli, leaves reserved, stems trimmed and halved lengthways

60 ml (2 fl oz/¼ cup) olive oil

1 small garlic clove, crushed

generous pinch of chilli flakes (or to taste)

3–4 tablespoons golden raisins, chopped, to serve

PARTY CRUNCH

60 g (2 oz/½ cup) sunflower kernels

3 tablespoons nutritional yeast flakes

½ cup fried shallots

¼ cup puffed rice

2 tablespoons chicken salt

BROWN BUTTER MAYO

170 g (6 oz) salted butter

2 tablespoons milk powder (only if you have it)

1 large egg yolk at room temp

2 teaspoons lemon juice

1 teaspoon cold water

SERVES 4–6

For the party crunch, combine all the ingredients in a bowl. Set aside.

For the brown butter mayo, melt the butter in a saucepan over a medium–low heat. Simmer until browned and foaming, then remove from the heat and whisk in the milk powder vigorously (if using). Set aside to cool. Put the egg yolk, lemon juice and cold water in a medium mixing bowl. Whisk until well-integrated and bright yellow. Now whisking constantly, add the brown butter in a very slow stream to the yolk mixture, literally a few drops at a time. You need it to start to emulsify, gradually adding the remaining butter until your mayonnaise is thick and spreadable. Taste and season with sea salt flakes and pepper.

Preheat the oven to 180°C (360°F). Line a large roasting tin with baking paper and lay the broccolini in a single layer. Mix the oil, garlic and chilli flakes together in a small bowl and brush over the broccolini, then season with sea salt flakes and freshly ground black pepper. Roast for 10–15 minutes or until the broccolini are tender and the edges browned.

To serve, smear the mayo on a plate, top with the broccoli halves and scatter over generous spoonfuls of the party crunch and the golden raisins.

HOT TIP Use this party crunch for any salad or fling it across roasted veg for an easy glow-up.

This is living

BROWN BUTTER GARLICKY MAC 'n' CHEESE

Mac 'n' cheese never used to be my thing. I'd constantly see it on menus but too often found myself struggling to swallow it, like I'm coming out the other side of a bad cold.

But a few little glow-ups – heavy on the garlic, browning the butter, very decent cheese – and this is get-in-my-mouth-I-can't-get-enough-of-it deliciousness.

Don't feel you have to use macaroni – any small pasta that loves things saucy will work.

500 ml (17 fl oz/2 cups) milk
4–6 fresh thyme stems
350 g (12½ oz) small pasta of your choice
75 g (2¾ oz) salted butter
5 garlic cloves, crushed
75 g (2¾ oz/½ cup) plain (all-purpose) flour
250 ml (8½ fl oz/1 cup) crème fraiche
100 g (3½ oz) gruyère, grated
100 g (3½ oz) smoked cheddar, grated
100 g (3½ oz) parmesan, grated
sliced mozzarella to finish (optional)

SERVES 4–6

Bring a large pot of water to a boil.

Meanwhile, in a separate saucepan, heat the milk and thyme over a low heat. You just want this to warm through, not boil, and the thyme to infuse it. Fish out the thyme stems and discard – no matter if a few leaves escape as they will only add to the flavour. Set aside.

Preheat the oven to 180°C (360°F).

Add your pasta to the pot of boiling water and cook until al dente. Reserve about a cup of the pasta water for the sauce, then drain the pasta and put in a bowl.

Return the pot you cooked your pasta in to the stove and add the butter. Let it cook over a low to medium heat until it darkens – you want it to smell nutty and look deep brown in colour, not black and burned. Remove from heat and add the garlic and give everything a good swirl – it will start cooking in the residual heat. Return to the stove and cook for another 30 seconds or so, then add the flour. Whisk briskly until the mixture comes away from the sides of the pan. Gradually add the infused milk, whisking to combine. Add the reserved pasta water and whisk again to incorporate. Stir through the crème fraiche and the cheeses. Keep stirring until the sauce thickens and coats the back of a spoon. Season with sea salt flakes and freshly ground pepper.

Add the cheesy sauce to the pasta, turning to coat. Pour into an ovenproof dish (or multiple small dishes) and top with slices of mozzarella. This is completely optional – I just love the oozy excessive nature of it, and in my mind, there is never too much cheese.

Pop in the oven and cook for 15 minutes. Turn the grill (broiler) to medium and grill until the tops look toasted and golden, anywhere between 3 and 5 minutes.

Season again with sea salt flakes and freshly cracked black pepper and serve.

Massive flavours. Greedy intent.

ROASTED TATERS, GOCHUJANG and CHIVE SOUR CREAM

Here is the great thing: these are wonderful for making friends. They are equally delightful on the couch with a bottle of plonk and a bad/good rom-com. A true friend with benefits.

If by chance (it's important in life to cover all bases) you have carb-averse friends and find yourself with leftovers, firstly find new friends, then blitz the lot in the blender and you've got the most marvellously decadent roast potato and gochujang soup. You're welcome.

Also, use any taters you have floating around. While I am very partial to a kipfler, I'd never suggest buying potatoes specially. Let's be honest: once they are hot and slicked in oil and roasted, they all taste good.

750 g (1 lb 11 oz) potatoes of choice, cut into bite-sized pieces (baby kipfler/fingerling potatoes halved lengthways recommended)

80 ml (2½ fl oz/⅓ cup) olive oil (or duck fat) for coating

GOCHUJANG AND CHIVE SOUR CREAM

300 ml (10 fl oz) sour cream

1 tablespoon gochujang paste (add gradually and test for heat)

very finely chopped chives, to serve

SERVES 6

Preheat the oven to 180°C (360°F).

To make the gochujang and chive sour cream, put all the ingredients in a bowl and stir to combine.

Put the potatoes in a roasting tin and drizzle over the oil. Toss to coat. If you don't think the potatoes are adequately coated, add a little more oil – this is not the time for caution and restraint. You don't want them swimming, but you do want your potatoes thoroughly coated. Season very generously with sea salt flakes and freshly ground black pepper and roast for 45 minutes or until golden and crisp.

Scoop the gochujang and chive sour cream into a serving bowl. Top with the potatoes, then season liberally with more sea salt flakes and freshly ground black pepper and scatter with the chives. Serve piping hot.

Gold plated goodness

BABA GHANOUSH, CHICKPEAS, CURRY LEAVES, PINE NUTS 'n' PITA

How good is burning the shit out of something and calling it delicious? This is smoky, easy and so, so good. Serve it with a bit of slow-cooked protein and a green salad for a dinner of dreams.

10 or so curry leaves

60 ml (2 fl oz/¼ cup) grapeseed oil

4 eggplants (aubergines) (about 1.3 kg/2 lb 14 oz), halved lengthways

2 tablespoons olive oil

2 garlic cloves, crushed

juice and zest of 1 lemon

1 teaspoon ground cumin

¼ cup each chopped mint and flat-leaf (Italian) parsley

200 g (7 oz) cooked chickpeas

toasted pine nuts, to serve

1–2 fluffy pita breads, toasted

SERVES 4–6

Preheat the oven to 200°C (390°F).

Heat the curry leaves and oil in a small frying pan over a high heat. Cook until the leaves curl and crisp, then immediately remove from the heat and set aside to cool.

Place the eggplant halves cut side up in a roasting tin and drizzle with the olive oil. Roast in the oven for 45 minutes, then turn the grill (broiler) to high and cook for a further 25 minutes or until you can smell it before you even open the oven door. It should have a caramelised, burned smell, and the eggplants should be very soft and the skin will resemble the leftovers of a fire.

Once cool enough to handle, scoop out the flesh of the eggplant halves and discard the skin. Pop the fleshy goodness into a strainer and set over the sink for 20 minutes to get rid of residual liquid.

Put the drained flesh in a bowl with the garlic, lemon juice and zest, cumin and chopped herbs and season with sea salt flakes and freshly ground black pepper. Mix together and give the mixture a quick pulse in a blender.

Smear the baba ghanoush over the base of a large bowl. Top with the chickpeas. Spoon over the curry leaves and oil, pine nuts and serve with the toasted pita.

Guest of honour
ROASTED PUMPKIN with HUMMUS and SPICY DATE CRUNCH

This is a zinging mess of caramelised roasted pumpkin, earthy dates and a slab of hummus with a crunch topper to remind us to chew.

1 kg (2 lb 3 oz) pumpkin (winter squash) cut into even-sized wedges, seeds removed

3 tablespoons olive oil

1 tablespoon maple syrup (optional)

150–200 g (5½–7 oz) hummus

chopped coriander (cilantro) and flat-leaf (Italian) parsley, to serve

DATE AND SPICE CRUNCH

6 dates, roughly chopped

1½ cups coarsely torn bite-sized chunks of day-old bread

3 tablespoons olive oil

1 tablespoon baharat spice blend (or any Middle Eastern spice blend wallowing in your spice drawer)

80 ml (2½ fl oz/⅓ cup) date syrup

SERVES 4–6

Preheat the oven to 180°C (360°F).

Add the pumpkin pieces to a roasting tin and drizzle over the oil and maple syrup (if using). Season with sea salt flakes and freshly ground black pepper and roast for 45 minutes or until caramelised, golden and cooked through.

When the pumpkin has about 15 minutes remaining, make the date and spice crunch by putting all the ingredients in a bowl and tossing to coat and incorporate. Spread over a baking tin lined with baking paper and roast in the oven until golden and toasted.

Spread the hummus over the base of a serving bowl. Arrange the pumpkin pieces on top and then scatter over the date and spice crunch. Sprinkle with the chopped herbs, season again with salt and pepper and serve.

Ode to the seagull
TOM'S HOT CHIPS

6 large potatoes such as Dutch or sebago

olive oil to generously coat

SEASONING MIX

2 tablespoons sea salt flakes, plus more to finish

1 tablespoon sweet smoked paprika

½ tablespoon each ground coriander, ground cumin, ground cardamom, dried oregano and dried thyme

SERVES 1. SERVES 4. (CHIP SERVES ARE IMPOSSIBLE TO QUANTIFY. WHEN IN DOUBT, ADD ANOTHER POTATO. YOU WON'T REGRET IT.)

My husband, Tom, is affectionately known as the seagull, and his love for a hot chip has been long, constant and unwavering. He will find that plate with a magician's sleight of hand, so fair to say he knows a good chip when he eats it. This is his treasured recipe. It's not a shoestring, but it's not a pub wedge; it sits happily in between, making them the perfect balance of crisp with pockets of potato innards that are soft and yielding. They are also done in the oven without any deep-frying shenanigans that just feel so labour-intensive and unnecessary at home.

Preheat the oven to 170°C (340°F).

Slice the potatoes into chips on a mandoline fitted with the serrated blade for cutting chips, otherwise cut with a knife. We're aiming for a 1 cm (½ in) thickness. Put them into a large bowl and cover with water. Set aside for 15 minutes before draining – they will look white and weird thanks to the starch.

Spread the chips out over a few large roasting tins.

Make the seasoning mix by putting the ingredients in a bowl and stirring to combine. Sprinkle over the chips, then use your hands to toss and coat. Drizzle over the olive oil (you want enough to thoroughly coat the chips) and toss again. Season generously with sea salt flakes.

Pop in the oven and cook for 45 minutes. Remove the trays and use a spatula to gently toss and spread the chips. Allow to cool for 15 minutes. This helps the chips to dry out and is a step you should try not to skip.

Meanwhile, increase the oven temperature to 220°C (430°F). Return the chips to the oven and cook for an additional 15 minutes or until the potato is cooked through and the chips look gloriously crisp.

A FEW IDEAS for FEEDING a CROWD

Having people over to eat is a lovely thing. It's the highest compliment to invite people into your home and take the time to cook for them. But you can't call people out after dark under false pretences. You do have to do the cooking bit, and the hosting bit, and the putting out the cutlery bit. And the washing up bit later, unless you can convince a few drunk late-night types to stay back and do it with you (advisable).

Below are some menu ideas for feeding a crowd. My biggest tip, if you are not a chef, is don't go trying to plate food. It's stressful, and the food gets cold waiting for you to pull out the tweezers. No one cares. Just plonk it on the table and enjoy the never-dying trend of share plates. It will make the whole process entirely more enjoyable. For you and them.

She's in a tizz; people are coming over

★ Bottle of plonk short ribs   168

★ Wedgie with tahini green dressing   172

★ Tom's hot chips   144

★ Roasted fennel with Café de Paris sauce   170

★ Blood plum pannacotta for a crowd with orange blossom and black pepper   222

Keeping it casual but still excellent

★ Massaman curried eggs   202

★ Pork burgers with red curry and coriander mayo   158

★ Black pepper beans   132

★ Turmeric lemongrass cold noodle salad   36

★ Liquorice chocolate brownie   186

Unexpected guests

★ Crudo 'n' crisps **166**

★ Lulu's Sunday night honey mustard chicken
drumsticks **80**

★ White bean and couscous salad
with roasted red pepper dressing **38**

★ Two-minute soft serve **226**

Somewhere in the middle

★ Real deal sour cream and onion dip
with non-negotiable Chicken Crimpies **198**

★ Jatz, tomato and harissa pie **160**

★ Bloody Mary's big balls
with fried pickles **58**

★ Slow-roasted cabbage
with madras curry butter **124**

★ Cabbage and kale slaw with chilli,
yeast and seed dressing **20**

★ One-bowl lemon cardamom
drizzle cake **180**

Winter feast

★ Herby lamb and date
slow-cooked goodness **118**

★ Sweet potato, kale and burghul salad
with chermoula cashew dressing **22**

★ Pumpkin with chickpea rice
and onions **162**

★ Baba ghanoush, chickpeas, curry leaves,
pine nuts 'n' pita **140**

★ Violet crumble for adults **218**

GOOD THINGS for WEEK- ENDS

Weekends are for really good things,
delightful and joyous things.

Weekends are for noisy tables. The clunk of
plates, the chink of glasses, the opening of
bottles and the buzzing of conversation
contrasted with the soft sounds of breaking
bread, passed dishes and murmurs of
enjoyment. Weekends present the
opportunity for fluidity. Meals can be enjoyed
at the stove, outside on the grass, at a bench,
on the boot of the car.

As a cook, these are the very moments
I live for. There is no greater reward.

These are the dishes for friends, for family, for
afternoons in the sun and for early evenings
that run long into the night. The opportunity
to enjoy them (the food and the people) is one
of life's greatest unsung luxuries.

Paradise found

STRADDIE PRAWN ROLLS

The world's greatest prawn rolls reside on Stradbroke Island. It's the kind of roll that is truly a gift from the gods. This is my interpretation.

You can double or triple this recipe depending on how many mouths you plan to feed. I'd always err on the side of more.

500 g (1 lb 2 oz) freshly cooked prawns (shrimp), cut into bite-sized pieces

90 g (3 oz/⅓ cup) Kewpie mayonnaise

½ teaspoon Worcestershire sauce

1 tablespoon tomato sauce (ketchup)

grated zest of 1 lemon

3 tablespoons chopped dill

1 large avocado, cut into chunks

fresh brioche rolls, baguette or whatever you can get your hands on

OPTIONAL EXTRAS

a crusting of dukkah

some fresh cos (romaine) lettuce for crunch

MAKES 4–5 ROLLS

Put the prawns, mayonnaise, Worcestershire sauce, tomato sauce, lemon zest and dill in a bowl and gently combine until the prawns are thoroughly coated. Add the avocado and season generously with sea salt flakes and cracked black pepper. Scoop into the fresh rolls and serve immediately.

These are best eaten just as they are made – there is nothing worse than a soggy-bottomed prawn roll. You want the squeak of prawn, the resistance of fresh, chewy bread and the general all-round amazing mouthfeel this combo supplies.

Eager to please

PIZZA and four GREAT TOPPINGS

As you get older, you realise the secret to happiness is the direct truth – say what you want in a partner, in bed, in your career and most definitely on your pizza.

This recipe is a hybrid – it flirts and dabbles between pizza and focaccia, and in my humble opinion it is the best of both worlds. You get moments of crust and crunch with spongy deliciousness, a textural wonderland. It is also completely consistent in results – oven, pizza oven or wood-fired oven, it works. Every. Single. Time.

7 g (¼ oz) dried yeast

2 tablespoons olive oil, plus extra for oiling

1 tablespoon honey

500 ml (17 fl oz/2 cups) tepid water

675 g (1½ lb) strong flour (I love Caputo flour)

2 teaspoons fine sea salt flakes

SERVES 8

Put the yeast, olive oil, honey and 375 ml (12½ fl oz/1½ cups) of tepid water in a jug. Set aside for 5–10 minutes until foaming and you see some little crater-like bubbles across the surface, like sea foam on a beach after a big storm.

Add, along with the flour and the salt, to the bowl of a stand mixer fitted with the dough hook. Add the yeast mixture and mix on medium for 5–8 minutes or until the dough is soft and elastic and starts to pull away from the sides of the bowl. It will still be somewhat sticky. If not, add additional water one tablespoon at a time. The amount of water needed can vary with temperature and the brand of flour used. Peel out the dough, add a drizzle of olive oil to the bowl and wipe it across the surface to give an oil coating. Return the dough to the bowl, cover with plastic wrap and pop in the fridge overnight. Alternatively, cover with a clean tea (dish) towel and let it sit for a few hours or until it has doubled in size.

Pull the dough from the fridge and let it come to room temperature. Turn out the dough and stretch to fit a large 40 × 28 cm (15¾ × 11 in) lipped baking tray that has been lightly greased with some olive oil, working the dough into the corners of the tray.

Preheat the oven to 220°C (430°F).

Let it rest again for 30 minutes or until you see bubbles here and there just under the surface.

Top with desired toppings. Cook for 20–25 minutes.

WHITE PIZZA

275 g (9½ oz) firm mozzarella, grated

250 g (9 oz/1 cup) smooth ricotta

185 ml (6 fl oz/¾ cup) thickened (whipping) cream

1 garlic clove, crushed

60 ml (2 fl oz/¼ cup) pizza sauce

1 tablespoon harissa paste (or to taste)

¾ cup dried olives

1 tablespoon toasted cumin seeds

60 ml (2 fl oz/¼ cup) olive oil

Combine the mozzarella, ricotta, cream and garlic in a bowl and spread over the pizza base. Combine the pizza sauce and harissa in a bowl then drizzle over the top of the pizza. Top with the dried olives and cumin seeds. Cook for 20–25 minutes, then drizzle with the olive oil, season with sea salt flakes and eat.

MORTY D and PISTACHIO

300 g (10½ oz) firm mozzarella, grated

100 g (3½ oz) sliced mortadella

basil leaves, to serve

drizzle of olive oil

QUICK PISTACHIO TOPPER

75 g (2 oz/½ cup) pistachios

grated zest of 1 lemon

olive oil as needed

Blitz the quick pistachio topper ingredients in a food processor until you get a chunky pesto texture. You will need to add olive oil until you get the consistency you want.

Spread the mozzarella over the pizza base and top with slices of mortadella. Cook for 20–25 minutes. Spoon over the pistachio topper and a few basil leaves and drizzle over some olive oil. Season with sea salt flakes and freshly ground black pepper. Eat.

SPINACH, POPPY SEEDS and HOT HONEY

185 ml (6 fl oz/¾ cup) pizza sauce

1 ball (approx. 125 g/4½ oz) buffalo mozzarella, sliced

2–3 tablespoons honey

generous pinch of Turkish red pepper flakes

2 tablespoons poppy seeds

100 g (3½ oz/2 cups) baby spinach

drizzle of olive oil

Spread the sauce over the pizza base and scatter the mozzarella slices. Shove in the oven for 20–25 minutes.

While the pizza is cooking, warm the honey in a small saucepan and add the Turkish red pepper flakes – taste and adjust to the heat you prefer. Add the poppy seeds.

When the pizza is bubbling and looks done, quickly cover the pizza in the spinach leaves and return to the oven to cook for another minute until the spinach has just wilted but is still a vibrant green. I tend to open the door and do the whole lot there without pulling from the oven, but this does come with a small risk of burning yourself.

Once the pizza is cooked, drizzle over the honey mixture and season with olive oil and salt.

OLIVE 'n' CURD PIZZA

185 ml (6 fl oz/¾ cup) pizza sauce

1 ball (approx. 125 g/4½ oz) buffalo mozzarella, sliced

125 g (4½ oz/1 cup) pitted black olives, chopped

150 g (5½ oz) ash-coated goat's cheese

1 cup deveined and coarsely torn young cavolo nero (Tuscan kale) leaves

drizzle of olive oil

Spread the sauce over the pizza base. Scatter the mozzarella slices, olives, goat's cheese and cavolo nero. Drizzle over a little olive oil and cook for 20–25 minutes. Season with sea salt flakes and freshly ground black pepper to serve.

Baked nafs

CHORIZO, PUMPKIN and KALE LASAGNE

Did you know that you can replace the words 'I tried really damn hard' with the word 'lasagne'? This is the cold, hard truth.

A properly made lasagne is proof you have the nafs. Derived from the Arabic word 'nafas', meaning 'breath' or 'spirit', it describes the most important ingredient – love. But in the context of cooking, nafs is more than that, an energy some people possess that makes their meals not just good but exceptional. I adore this sentiment to describe the very essence of anything ever done in a home kitchen.

This lasagne is my addled version of the world's greatest lasagne by Elizabeth Hewson, incorporating a hit of smoky chorizo heat and some salty olives for contrast.

850 g (1 lb 14 oz) pumpkin (winter squash), seeds and skin removed, cut into thin 1 cm (½ in) wedges

3 tablespoons olive oil, plus extra for drizzling

800 g (1 lb 12 oz) tinned finely chopped tomatoes

¼ cup chopped basil leaves, plus some whole leaves to serve

125 ml (4 fl oz/½ cup) stock

½ tablespoon brown sugar

6 fresh chorizo sausages (approx. 600 g/1 lb 5 oz), skins removed, meat roughly chopped

6 garlic cloves, finely diced

leaves of 1 small bunch cavolo nero (Tuscan kale), chopped

grated zest of 1 lemon

60 g (2 oz/½ cup) pitted black olives, chopped

800 g (1 lb 12 oz) fresh lasagne sheets

200 g (7 oz) firm mozzarella, grated

100 g (3½ oz) smoked cheddar, grated

BECHAMEL

800 ml (27 fl oz) milk

1 bay leaf

2 rosemary sprigs

80 g (2¾ oz) salted butter

80 g (2¾ oz) plain (all-purpose) flour

2 garlic cloves, crushed

100 g (3½ oz) parmesan, grated

pinch of ground nutmeg

white pepper

SERVES 8–10

Preheat the oven to 190°C (375°F). Spread the pumpkin slices in a single layer across a large roasting tin lined with baking paper. Drizzle over 2 tablespoons of the oil and season with sea salt flakes and freshly ground black pepper. Roast for 30 minutes or until golden and cooked through.

Put the tomatoes into a medium saucepan. Add the basil, stock and sugar and simmer on a very low heat for the remainder of the time the pumpkin is cooking,

Place a frying pan over a medium heat. Add the remaining oil and, once hot, throw in the chorizo and cook until crisping on the edges and the oil is starting to leach from the meat into the pan. Add the garlic and fry until fragrant. Add the cavolo nero and lemon zest and cook until just softened. Remove, stir through the olives and set aside.

For the bechamel, warm the milk in a small saucepan and add the bay leaf and rosemary. Set aside to infuse for about 10 minutes. Strain and discard the bay leaf and rosemary sprigs. Melt the butter in a saucepan over a medium heat. Add the flour and cook for 1 minute, stirring constantly. Gradually add the infused milk, stirring constantly. Add the garlic and continue stirring until it thickly coats the back of a wooden spoon. Remove from the stove and add the parmesan and nutmeg, then season with salt and white pepper. Cover with a lid and keep warm.

When ready to assemble, quickly blanch the lasagne sheets in a pot of boiling water for 30 seconds, then lay on baking paper and drizzle with a little olive oil to prevent sticking.

Rub the sides of a 3-litre (101 fl oz/12 cups) ovenproof dish generously with olive oil. Line the base with pasta sheets, trimming if needed. Top with a layer of roasted pumpkin pieces and scatter over a little of the cavolo nero and chorizo mixture. Pour over just enough tomato sauce to cover and sprinkle over some mozzarella and cheddar. Add just enough bechamel to cover, then repeat with remaining pasta and filling for three to four layers in total. When you get to your last one or two layers, leave some pasta overhanging; this crisps beautifully in the oven. And make sure you are generous with the bechamel and cheese for the very top layer for golden melty goodness. I like to put the cheese on top of the bechamel here for maximum bubbling golden deliciousness.

Pop in the oven and cook for 40–50 minutes until bubbling and golden and the overhanging lasagne sheets are crisp and irresistible.

From scratch

PORK BURGERS
with
RED CURRY
and
CORIANDER MAYO

This is a case of delayed gratification. You need to simmer it on the stove and know it will have nothing interesting to say for a good few hours. But, oh, when it's ready, it has some very good things to say indeed. It's the kind of slow cook that results in soft pork that could well vaporise at the sight of a fork.

This is perfect weekend fodder – soft buns brimming with tasty moreish goodness, like an overstuffed pouf in the living room. It covers all manner of meals from morning to dusk, plates and cutlery always optional.

2 tablespoons olive oil

1.7 kg (3 lb 12 oz) pork collar butt (shoulder), cut into large chunks

⅓ cup finely chopped ginger

8 garlic cloves, grated

2 lemongrass stems, white part only, finely chopped

BRAISING LIQUID

60 ml (2 fl oz/¼ cup) salt-reduced soy sauce

125 ml (4 fl oz/½ cup) dark sweet soy (kecap manis)

60 ml (2 fl oz/¼ cup) oyster sauce

325 ml (11 fl oz) salt-reduced chicken stock

115 g (4 oz/½ cup) brown sugar

RED CURRY MAYO

125 g (4½ oz/½ cup) Kewpie mayonnaise

½–1 teaspoon red curry paste

2–3 tablespoons finely chopped coriander (cilantro)

TO SERVE

finely sliced cabbage or cos (romaine) lettuce

brioche buns

coriander (cilantro), mint and Thai basil leaves (optional)

SERVES 8–10

Heat the olive oil in a large stockpot. Once shimmering, add the pork and fry until browned all over. Add the ginger, garlic and lemongrass and cook until fragrant.

Put the braising liquid ingredients in a bowl along with 125 ml (4 fl oz/½ cup) water and stir to combine. Pour the liquid over the pork, bring to a simmer and cook for 3 hours, lid off, stirring every 30 minutes or so until the pork is soft and the sauce has thickened and looks superbly glossy. Allow to cool slightly before going at it with a pair of forks and shredding the pork into saucy oblivion.

For the red curry mayo, combine all the ingredients in a bowl. Taste and adjust for heat with more curry paste if you like.

To assemble, layer some cabbage or lettuce on warmed brioche buns. Top with generous spoonfuls of pork and finish with the red curry mayo and herbs, if using.

HOT TIP Ensure you use low-salt soy and stock to ensure this doesn't have you sculling cups of water for days afterwards.

JATZ, TOMATO and HARISSA PIE

Cheese and a cracker, but elevated. Because that is how we roll.

Now you might be the type that skips reading the instructions and heads straight to the set-up. STOP. I really want you to take this on board: to ensure this is a firm tart, you really want to take your time compacting the biscuit base – it will add a minute to your labour time but will result in a delightful crust that doesn't collapse. Put your back into it. Worth it.

1 kg (2 lb 3 oz) medium tomatoes

olive oil for drizzling

225 g (8 oz) Jatz crackers (if Jatz unavailable, substitute with Ritz crackers)

1 teaspoon garlic powder

1 egg plus 1 yolk

125 g (4½ oz) salted butter, melted

fried garlic slices, to serve (optional)

CHEESY LAYER

½ cup grated manchego

½ cup grated fontina

¼ cup soft goat's cheese

½ teaspoon each ground caraway, ground cumin and ground coriander

1 egg

1 tablespoon harissa paste (or to taste)

SERVES 10

Preheat your oven to 170°C (340°F).

Slice the tomatoes evenly and spread on a roasting tin lined with baking paper (you might need two). Drizzle with a little olive oil and season generously with sea salt flakes. Pop in the oven and cook for 40 minutes or until the tomatoes have roasted and dried out a bit.

Grease a 22 cm (8¾ in) fluted tart tin with a removable base. Line the base with baking paper. Put the crackers, garlic powder and a big pinch of sea salt flakes in a food processor and blitz to very fine crumbs. Add the egg plus extra yolk and the melted butter to the cracker crumbs and blitz again until it comes together. It should resemble wet sand and almost clump in the food processor. Tip the mixture into the centre of your tart tin, pressing it down across the base and up the sides. Using the flat base of a glass, start in the centre and work outward, pressing very firmly on the bottom. When you reach the sides, place your thumb over the top of the crumb edge, pressing down on the crumbs at the same time as you are pushing the glass up against the sides. Do not rush this step! You want to compact the mixture as firmly and evenly as possible.

Pop the tart tin on a baking tray, then shove it in the oven and bake for 8–10 minutes. Remove and allow to cool.

For the cheesy layer, combine all the ingredients in a bowl. Dollop half the cheesy mixture over the cooled tart base. Layer over half the roasted tomatoes, then top again with the rest of the cheese mixture and finish with the remaining tomatoes. Pop back into the oven to cook for 1 hour.

When it's done, you need to be patient and let this cool, because cutting while it is still hot will mean a crumbly mess – trust me, I know. Patience, in this case, is a very good thing. Once cooled, use a sharp knife to cut into slices. Scatter with fried garlic, if using, just before serving.

Gold-fleshed goodness
PUMPKIN with CHICKPEA RICE and ONIONS

When the food is also the vessel.

I love the hole in one this kind of cooking provides. While you will have to get very, very intimate with your pumpkin, shaving and scraping to fill it with the goods, it is after that point a very hands-off cook, and the alchemy emerging from your oven is nothing but victorious.

1 small-medium (about 1.6 kg/ 3½ lb) kent pumpkin (winter squash)

100 ml (3½ fl oz) olive oil

4 brown onions, sliced

2 garlic cloves, crushed

80 g (2¾ oz/½ cup) pine nuts

75 g (2¾ oz/½ cup) currants

450 g (1 lb/2½ cups) cooked brown rice

400 g (14 oz) tinned chickpeas, drained and rinsed

½ tablespoon each ground cumin and ground coriander

2 teaspoons pomegranate molasses (optional)

60 ml (2 fl oz/¼ cup) vegetable stock

2 tablespoons maple syrup

TAHINI YOGHURT

250 g (9 oz/1 cup) Greek yoghurt

2 tablespoons tahini

juice of 1 small lemon

1 garlic clove, crushed

pinch of ground cumin

½ cup coriander leaves, chopped, plus extra to scatter

SERVES 6-8

Preheat the oven to 180°C (360°F).

Use a sharp knife to cut off the top of the pumpkin – this will become your lid, so you want this to be approximately 5–8 cm (2–3¼ in) thick, to hold its shape when cooked. Set aside. Using your knife, cut around from the open top down into the inside of the pumpkin to remove the seeds and fibrous 'pumpkin brains' – it will feel quite tough against the knife cutting into the uncooked pumpkin flesh. Discard seeds and pulp. If you had a relatively small amount of pulp and seeds, you may need to cut and remove a layer of pumpkin flesh so the fillings fit into your pumpkin.

Place the pumpkin on a large roasting tin lined with baking paper and set aside while you prepare the filling.

Place a frying pan over a low heat. Add 2 tablespoons of the oil and, once hot, fry the onions, stirring regularly for up to 15 minutes or until soft. Add the garlic, pine nuts and currants and fry for another 2 minutes. Add the rice, chickpeas, spices and pomegranate molasses and give it all a good turn to combine. Season with sea salt flakes and freshly cracked black pepper.

Spoon the mixture into the pumpkin. If it feels like it's overflowing, gently press down to compact the mixture. Pour in the stock then place the lid of the pumpkin on top. Drizzle over the remaining olive oil and the maple syrup. Roast in the oven for 1½–2 hours or until the pumpkin is completely cooked through.

Make the tahini yoghurt by combining all the ingredients in a bowl. If it tastes too tart, add a teaspoon of maple syrup. Season with sea salt flakes.

Remove the top of the cooked pumpkin and drizzle with the tahini yoghurt.

To serve, use a knife to make an incision into the pumpkin to cut into a wedge of sorts, or simply let people use a spoon to scoop filling and pumpkin flesh onto their plates.

Time to unwind
The SUNDAY SAUCE

3 tablespoons olive oil

1 onion, diced

100 g (3½ oz) guanciale or speck, diced

8 garlic cloves, chopped

450 g (1 lb) Italian sausage, skin removed and meat chopped

450 g (1 lb) pork spare ribs

450 g (1 lb) steak, chopped

60 g (2 oz/¼ cup) tomato paste (concentrated purée)

2.4 kg (5 lb 7 oz) tinned whole tomatoes, crushed with your hands

3 tablespoons chopped oregano

3 tablespoons chopped basil

1 parmesan rind

pinch of caster (superfine) sugar

pasta of your choice, to serve

SERVES 12

Sunday sauce is how you make your house smell like a home. People on their afternoon walks will pause as they pass to inhale the smells of slow-cooked goodness and comfort wafting from the windows, their dogs salivating silver trails across your path.

This is not food for the frenetic, harried way we live now – like an endangered culture, this is slow and meaningful and measured. It is equal parts frugality and 'fill your cup' sentimentality in a sauce.

The key to success is the long simmer and using up whatever bits and bobs of meat you have on hand. Traditionally it's a mix of three or so meats; throw in a combination of whatever you have on hand and ideally some form of meat on the bone for maximum flavour. And according to my Italian friends, heavily involved in the research, there is also always some form of pork for ultimate flavour.

You could use some butcher fire-sale meat that is still good but needs to be moved on. Whatever you find, it is always delicious. Just don't rush it.

Put the oil in a stockpot and place over a medium heat. Once hot, throw in the onion and cook until soft and translucent. Add the guanciale and garlic and fry until fragrant and the guanciale is looking crisp. Add the meat in batches and brown thoroughly on all sides. Add the tomato paste and cook until darkened and it looks like it is coming away from the edges of the pot, about 1 minute. Add the tomatoes along with 250 ml (8½ fl oz/ 1 cup) of water, the herbs and the parmesan rind. Simmer uncovered for a minimum of 3 hours, but 5 hours is best, giving it the occasional stir. You can add more water if it's looking too thick or you are concerned it has reduced too rapidly. Alternatively, if your sauce doesn't appear to have thickened, just turn up the heat slightly and cook a little longer.

Remove from the heat and take out the bones. I find it easiest to fish the pork ribs out, pull the meat from the bones and chuck it back into the pot, stirring well. Using a couple of forks, shred all the meat in the sauce – you are looking for a ragu-style consistency. Season with a pinch of caster sugar, salt and pepper. I like to leave the parmesan rind in – it's like a love note to the meal about to be devoured.

Serve with pasta.

GOOD THINGS FOR WEEKENDS

Fish 'n' chips of sorts

CRUDO 'n' CRISPS

This is 150 per cent my favourite way to eat, one I'll never tire of.

This is made for hot summer holiday afternoons and cold beers and is possibly the greatest weekend grazing snack in all of the lands. Forever and ever. The End.

Use excellent potato chips or you are dead to me.

½ teaspoon yuzu kosho
juice and zest of ½ lime
125 g (½ oz/½ cup) Kewpie mayonnaise
1 avocado, cubed
250 g (9 oz) sashimi-grade tuna, cut into 1 cm (½ in) cubes
3 tablespoons very finely chopped chives, plus extra to serve
excellent plain potato chips (crisps), to serve

SERVES 4–6 AS A SNACK

Combine the yuzu kosho, lime juice and zest and mayonnaise in a bowl. You want the consistency to be thinner than mayonnaise but thicker than water, so adjust with more lime juice or mayonnaise as needed or to your preferred taste – it needs to be easy to coat. Add the avocado, sashimi and chives and turn gently with a spoon to coat. Season generously with sea salt flakes and freshly ground black pepper.

Turn out onto a serving plate, top with a little extra chive action and serve with a really excellent bag of crisps.

BOTTLE of PLONK SHORT RIBS

The meat just tumbles off into the saucy depths. It's a feat and one you have to do very little for. Mark these as very good, with a gold star and a tick. They deliver that perfect Sunday feeling of food-comfort euphoria.

2 kg (4 lb 6 oz) beef short ribs (or other secondary beef cut) at room temperature

flour for dredging (about ½ cup)

80 ml (2½ fl oz/⅓ cup) olive oil

2 large onions, finely chopped

2 carrots, peeled and chopped

1 large celery stalk, finely diced

3 rosemary stems

3 thyme stems

3 tarragon stems

2 garlic bulbs, trimmed of excess outer peel and halved

750 ml (25½ fl oz/3 cups) red wine

750 ml (25½ fl oz/3 cups) beef stock (use veal jus in there if you are feeling flush)

3 tablespoons brown sugar

generous knob of butter

SERVES 8

Preheat the oven to 175°C (345°F).

Once you've recovered from chopping all the vegetables, dredge your beef short ribs in the flour – dust off so they are only lightly covered.

Add the olive oil to an ovenproof stockpot with a lid and place over a medium heat. Once hot, add the ribs and sear on all sides. Remove to a plate then add the vegetables to the pan. Turn the heat to low and fry until soft and translucent, stirring regularly. Don't be in a hurry here – at least 10–12 minutes on a super low heat is where the magic will happen.

Return the ribs to the pan and add the herbs and heads of garlic. Play a bit of Tetris to make it all fit in snugly, then pour over the wine and beef stock. Let it get acquainted for 10 or so minutes before putting the lid on and transferring to the oven. Cook for 4 hours. (I like to check how it is reducing at the 2½ hour mark. You want to ensure the ribs are submerged in the liquid and that it isn't reducing too rapidly.)

After 4 hours, pull from the oven and carefully remove the ribs to a plate. Strain the sauce to remove the chunky bits and discard the latter except for the garlic – squeeze out the gloriously soft cloves into the sauce.

Return the sauce to the stockpot over a medium heat. Add the brown sugar and butter and simmer until the sauce has thickened and would easily coat the back of a spoon. This can take up to 20 minutes. Return the ribs to the sauce to warm through before serving. Season generously with sea salt flakes and freshly ground black pepper.

Heaven on a plate

ROASTED
FENNEL
with
CAFÉ DE PARIS SAUCE

This was such a happy accident, like the best cooking trials often are. The sauce is of course multi-use – I imagine it being equally content poured over a bistecca hot from the grill as being the bath for this slow-roasted fennel. The combination is what dreams are made of.

2 fennel bulbs, trimmed and quartered (halve again if very large)

80 ml (2½ fl oz/⅓ cup) olive oil

CAFÉ DE PARIS SAUCE

50 g (1¾ oz) salted butter

1 French shallot, finely diced

2 garlic cloves, crushed

2 anchovies

1 teaspoon mild curry powder

pinch of paprika

1 teaspoon dijon mustard

125 ml (4 fl oz/½ cup) pouring (single) cream

3 teaspoons very finely chopped flat-leaf (Italian) parsley

2 teaspoons tarragon leaves, finely sliced

1 tablespoon capers

**SERVES 4–6
AS PART OF A SPREAD**

Preheat the oven to 160°C (320°F).

Put the fennel quarters in a roasting tin and drizzle over the olive oil. Season with sea salt flakes and freshly ground black pepper. Roast in the oven for 1½ hours or until the fennel is very tender and caramelised.

To make the Café de Paris sauce, put the butter in a small frying pan and place over a low heat. Once foaming, fry the chopped French shallot until soft. Add the garlic and anchovies and cook until the garlic is fragrant and the anchovies seem to have melted into oblivion. Add the curry powder and paprika and cook until the mixture seems coated, then add the mustard and cream and stir constantly for a few minutes. It should thicken and reduce slightly. Season with sea salt and black pepper. Just before serving, add the herbs and capers and stir to combine. (If you are making this ahead of time, make sure to cool the sauce slightly then cover in a piece of plastic wrap to prevent a skin from forming. Gently reheat before serving.)

To serve, pour the Café de Paris sauce onto a serving plate. Place the roasted fennel pieces on top, season with sea salt flakes and serve warm.

HOT TIP This sauce is glorious with roasted celeriac and even tossed through noodles. And, of course, poured over a steak, but that feels far too obvious to say.

Pure summer

WEDGIE with TAHINI GREEN DRESSING

Lettuce that tastes like a glass of water, fresh herbs and the crunch of radishes. Spring and summer greens on a plate.

As far as the dressing goes, the tahini is present but not overwhelming as it too often is, when everything gets lost to a mouthfeel coating of sesame. It knows its place here, and this salad is all the better for it. Also it takes mere seconds to throw together, so that's another strong plus.

---

4 cos (romaine) lettuces, washed and quartered

2 radishes, finely sliced

¼ telegraph (long) cucumber, thinly sliced

2 avocados, quartered

juice of ½ lemon

drizzle of olive oil

TAHINI GREEN DRESSING

125 ml (4 fl oz/½ cup) buttermilk

125 g (4½ oz/½ cup) Kewpie mayonnaise

65 g (2¼ oz/¼ cup) tahini

½ cup each of flat-leaf (Italian) parsley and dill

SERVES 4–6

To make the dressing, whizz all the ingredients in a food processor to combine. Season with sea salt flakes and freshly ground black pepper.

Arrange the lettuce quarters on a large platter. Layer over the radish, cucumber and avocado. Spoon over the dressing.

Season with the lemon juice, a drizzle of olive oil and some salt and pepper before serving.

HOT TIP This dressing wants to be on all the crisp green things, is great smeared alongside a steak, and never met a tin of chickpeas it didn't like – turn through a tin or two for a light meal or blitz together for a pretty great snack dip.

My kind of taco

The CRISPIEST of CRISPY PRAWN TACOS with (not) DRUNK MAYO

Just when you thought the salad on the back of the packet was the only thing you could do with a packet of Chang's, think again. It makes the most perfect, crunchy, crispy prawn coating imaginable for this take on tacos, sans any kind of deep-fry.

Here for it. Your weekend should be too.

Also, the mayo isn't drunk – I just wanted to get you this far. It's a mere sniff, one that can be easily omitted if you are concerned about alcoholic dip, which no one should be. Ever.

60 g (2 oz/2 cups) cornflakes

150 g (5½ oz/1 cup) Chang's fried noodles

2 tablespoons nutritional yeast flakes

1 tablespoon garlic powder

1 tablespoon sweet smoked paprika

1 large egg

1 teaspoon gochujang paste

flour for dredging (about ½ cup)

250 g (9 oz) peeled and deveined green prawns (shrimp) (I prefer to use small prawns here)

drizzle of olive oil

(NOT) DRUNK MAYO

1 tablespoon sake

1 tablespoon sweet soy

grated zest of 1 lime

1–3 teaspoons gochujang (depending on how you like your heat)

180 g (6½ oz/¾ cup) Kewpie mayonnaise

TO SERVE

soft corn tortillas

cos (romaine) lettuce

1–2 avocados, sliced

chopped coriander (cilantro) leaves and spring onions (scallions)

lime wedges

MAKES 8–10 TACOS

Preheat the oven to 185°C (365°F) and line a large roasting tin with baking paper.

To make the mayo, whisk everything in a small bowl and set aside until ready to serve.

Blitz the cornflakes, fried noodles, yeast flakes, garlic powder and paprika in a food processor until you have a very chunky crumb. You don't want to make breadcrumbs, it needs a bit of life and texture – that's where the golden crisp resides.

Whisk the egg and gochujang together in a bowl, then set up a prep station with a bowl of flour, the egg mixture and the cornflake mixture in a third bowl.

Dredge your prawns in the flour, shaking them off before giving a quick dip in the egg mixture and then coating in the cornflake mixture. Place the coated prawns on your prepared tray and repeat with remaining prawns and mixture.

Drizzle some olive oil over the coated prawns and put in the oven for 8 minutes. Turn the grill (broiler) function to medium–low and give it another minute to get some extra crisp on the top of the prawns.

To serve, warm your tortillas then layer each with some cos, avocado, coriander and spring onion and top with the prawns. Drizzle over the spicy mayo and give everything a hose down in lime juice. Eat as fast as you can so you can make another one before anyone else.

BAKING

BENDERS

The following recipes are hedonism in baked form. I am aware there are people out there making brownies from sweet potatoes and black beans and all manner of things, but I will never understand gussying up a treat to be anything other than what it is – the whole 'healthy treat' misnomer is enough to slacken my jaw from the rest of my head.

If you want to be healthy, dive deeply into all the vegetables and fruit you like, staying away from chapters like these. But if, like me, you consider baked delights as something to make, look forward to, gift or savour in all their sugar-crusted goodness, then the following recipes are for you (and me).

I also don't think that baking should be about perfection. I adore robust cakes, fillings that ooze and crumbs that form. Let's delight in the fact that there is cake, or a slice or a wedge of something, baked with love and care, and not worry about the fruit that may have sunk, the corner that is slightly burned or that the mouthfeel of the crumb is not quite what we had hoped. Because to everyone else, it will taste amazing. That's when it really comes to life.

Bliss in baked form

SPICED APPLE CRUMBLE SLAB CAKE of YOUR DREAMS™

The best cake I have ever made. The End.

True story: if apple crumble and apple pie could leave a note on a spiced cake's dash saying, 'Call me, we're pregnant,' this is that moment. A complex, intriguing and entirely beguiling love tryst of baked-good goodness.

It's cake, it's pie, it's crumble, and they are working together to make the cake-eating world a better place.

500 g (1 lb 2 oz) plain (all-purpose) flour

480 g (1 lb 1 oz) caster (superfine) sugar

2½ tablespoons baking powder

generous pinch of salt

265 g (9½ oz) unsalted butter, cubed

4 extra-large eggs

300 ml (10 fl oz) buttermilk

2 tablespoons ground cinnamon

1 teaspoon each ground cloves and ground cardamom

2 tablespoons vanilla bean paste

6 granny smith apples, peeled, cored and cut into 1 cm (½ in) cubes

2 tablespoons brown sugar

CRUMBLE TOPPING

200 g (7 oz) plain (all-purpose) flour

85 g (3 oz) caster (superfine) sugar

85 g (3 oz) brown sugar

1 tablespoon ground cinnamon

½ teaspoon ground cardamom

190 g (6½ oz) unsalted butter, cubed

50 g (1¾ oz/½ cup) rolled (porridge) oats

3 tablespoons raw (demerara) sugar

**SERVES 12–14
(OR 1 FOR A FEW DAYS)**

Preheat the oven to 180°C (360°F) and line a 30 × 23 × 5 cm (12 × 9 × 2 in) baking tin with baking paper.

For the crumble mixture, combine all the ingredients in a bowl. Use your fingers to work the butter through the mixture until you get a rough crumb. Set aside.

Put the flour, sugar, baking powder and salt in the bowl of an electric mixer. Beat in the butter a few cubes at a time until it looks like a fine crumble – this can take a few minutes. Add the eggs and beat until incorporated. Add the buttermilk, 1 tablespoon of the ground cinnamon, the ground cloves and cardamom, and 1 tablespoon of the vanilla bean paste and beat until incorporated then continue to beat on high until the mixture is smooth and combined – it will seem a bit lighter and fluffier. Scrape the mixture into the baking tin and bake for 20 minutes.

Put the diced apples in a bowl with the brown sugar and the remaining tablespoons of ground cinnamon and vanilla bean paste and give them a quick toss to coat.

At the 20-minute mark, working quickly, open the oven and gently scatter the apple mixture in an even layer across the top of the sponge. Bake for another 15 minutes.

Open the oven and scatter the crumble mixture over the top of the apple mixture. Bake for another 20 minutes or until a skewer inserted in the centre comes out mostly clean.

Leave in the tin to cool before cutting into glorious, serious chunks of cake.

Casual yet decadent

One-BOWL LEMON CARDAMOM DRIZZLE CAKE

Cake for one or cake for many: if I could endure pain, I would have this mantra tattooed somewhere unspeakable.

This is so easy, and the little chunks of lemon flesh throughout add the necessary tang and intrigue to make this a rather sensational little cake.

260 g (9 oz/1¾ cups) plain (all-purpose) flour

1 teaspoon baking powder

½ teaspoon bicarbonate of soda (baking soda)

1 teaspoon freshly ground cardamom

pinch of fine sea salt flakes

juice and zest of 2 lemons

230 g (8 oz/1 cup) caster (superfine) sugar

2 teaspoons vanilla bean paste

185 ml (6 fl oz/¾ cup) light olive oil

125 g (4½ oz/½ cup) Greek yoghurt

2 large eggs

flesh of ½ lemon, seeds removed, finely chopped

dried edible rose petals to scatter

GLAZE

1 teaspoon freshly ground cardamom

juice of 2 small lemons

155 g (5½ oz/1¼ cups) icing (confectioners') sugar (or more as needed)

SERVES 8–10

Preheat the oven to 170°C (340°F) and grease and line a 20 cm (8 in) square cake tin.

In a large bowl, whisk together the flour, baking powder, bicarbonate of soda, cardamom and salt and set aside.

Massage the lemon zest into the sugar then stir into the flour mixture. In a large pouring jug, add the lemon juice, vanilla bean paste, olive oil, yoghurt and eggs, whisking to combine. Add the chopped lemon flesh to the ingredients in the jug and whisk again.

Pour the mixture into the flour mix and whisk until just combined and there are no clumps, but be careful not to overmix here. Scrape the batter into the cake tin and bake for 30–40 minutes or until golden and cooked through. Allow to cool.

To make the glaze, whisk together the cardamom, lemon juice and icing sugar in a bowl. If you have a lot of lumps, let it sit for a bit as the sugar will dissolve in the lemon juice, then whisk again until smooth. Drizzle the glaze over the cooled cake to your liking, scatter over the rose petals and serve.

The ultimate tea dunker

BROWNED-BUTTER MILO, MALT 'n' MISO BISCUITS

This is the right amount of crisp and chew. I want a cookie that can bend (the chew) to my pressure while putting up a fight (the crisp). The miso, the malt, the Milo – possibly the most perfect ménage à trois.

For a peak biscuit experience, make the dough then pop it in the fridge overnight before baking.

125 g (4½ oz) unsalted butter

150 g (5½ oz) brown sugar

50 g (1¾ oz) caster (superfine) sugar

3 tablespoons liquid malt

1 large egg

2 tablespoons white miso

2 teaspoons vanilla bean paste

60 g (2 oz/¼ cup) Milo, plus 1 tablespoon extra for the topping

220 g (8 oz/1¾ cups) plain (all-purpose) flour

½ teaspoon baking powder

pinch of fine salt flakes

200 g (7 oz/1 generous cup) milk chocolate chunks

generous pinch of salt flakes, to serve

MAKES APPROXIMATELY 20 BISCUITS (COOKIES)

Line a large baking tray with baking paper.

Put the butter in a saucepan over a medium heat until it foams and starts to turn brown. You will see some black flecks and it will have a lovely nutty aroma. Set aside to cool.

Once cool to the touch, put the browned butter in a mixing bowl with both the sugars and the malt and whisk until no lumps remain. Add the egg, miso and vanilla bean paste and whisk again until the mixture looks nice and glossy.

In a separate bowl, combine the Milo, flour, baking powder and salt. Fold these dry ingredients through the butter miso mixture until combined. Fold through the chocolate chunks.

Using a biscuit scoop or dessert spoon, scoop into balls and space them out on the lined tray, then pop in the fridge. It is best if you can leave them overnight or for 1 hour at a minimum.

Preheat the oven to 175°C (345°F).

Remove from the fridge and bake for 10 minutes. Remove from the oven and, while the biscuits are still soft, gently press down on them with the back of a flat spatula. Sprinkle over the extra Milo and a generous smattering of sea salt. Leave to cool, if you can, before eating at speed.

Heaven-sent (in a cake)

A VERY, VERY DEPENDABLE CHOCOLATE CAKE

Everyone needs a dependable chocolate cake. One that covers all types of occasions and emotional needs.

This is my favourite party cake, and it hangs on the quality of your cocoa powder. Of all your baking ingredients, this is KEY. Cocoa powder should always be Dutch-processed.

The cake-to-icing ratio is just as it should be. One to one.

425 g (15 oz) plain (all-purpose) flour

150 g (5½ oz) Dutch (unsweetened) cocoa powder (A-grade good stuff)

1 teaspoon bicarbonate of soda (baking soda)

1 tablespoon baking powder

pinch of salt

625 g (1 lb 6 oz) caster (superfine) sugar

3 large eggs

250 ml (8½ fl oz/1 cup) olive oil

300 g (10½ oz) sour cream

250 ml (8½ fl oz/1 cup) buttermilk

125 ml (4 fl oz/½ cup) hot water (you can add coffee in place of the water if you wish, I just always think I can taste it)

BUTTERCREAM ICING

6 egg whites

200 g (7 oz) caster (superfine) sugar

325 g (11½ oz) unsalted butter, diced, at room temperature

2–3 tablespoons sifted Dutch (unsweetened) cocoa powder (or more, depending on how rich you like it)

pinch of salt

edible flowers, to serve (optional)

SERVES 12

Preheat the oven to 170°C (340°F) and grease and line a 30 × 23 cm (12 × 9 in) baking tin.

Put the flour, cocoa, bicarbonate of soda, baking powder, salt and caster sugar in a large mixing bowl. Whisk to fully incorporate.

Put the eggs, olive oil, sour cream and buttermilk in a jug and whisk until smooth. Stream this gradually into the bowl of dry ingredients, whisking constantly in the same direction until the mixture is thick, smooth and glossy. Slowly whisk in the hot water.

Pour the batter into the lined baking tin and bake for 30 minutes or until a skewer inserted in the middle comes out clean. Set aside to cool.

For the buttercream icing, put the egg whites and caster sugar in the bowl of an electric mixer and set it over a saucepan of simmering water. Whisk constantly until it reaches 160°C (320°F). If you don't have a sugar thermometer, just whisk and keep touching the bowl – as soon as it feels like it would burn your finger if you held it there a moment longer, it should be about ready. The sugar should have completely dissolved into the egg white and the mixture should look like a clear kind of glue.

Immediately remove the bowl and set it on the electric mixer fitted with the whisk attachment. Whisk on high speed until a thick and glossy meringue has formed, 5–7 minutes. Switch out the whisk for the paddle attachment and beat in the butter, a tablespoon at a time, until it is all used up. Lower the speed and slowly add the cocoa powder along with a pinch of salt until incorporated. Taste and add more cocoa powder if you like. Continue to beat until silky, smooth and aerated.

Spread the icing liberally over the top of the cooled cake. Don't try to be neat – the more peaks and troughs, the more glorious it looks. Top with a pinch of sea salt flakes and some edible flowers if you fancy.

The mother of all brownies
LIQUORICE CHOCOLATE BROWNIE

This is nothing more than my compulsion to indulge. Brownie is crack to me, a kryptonite I cannot say no to. Ditto for liquorice. And this combo is the kind of perversion my mouth cannot say no to. The liquorice through and on the brownie makes this chewy, crispy and properly indulgent. It is excellence in baked form.

450 g (1 lb) soft, excellent-quality liquorice

280 g (10 oz) unsalted butter

200 g (7 oz) caster (superfine) sugar

300 g (10½ oz) brown sugar

5 eggs

125 g (4½ oz) Dutch (unsweetened) cocoa powder

generous pinch of salt

115 g (4 oz) plain (all-purpose) flour

sea salt flakes, to finish

SERVES 12

Preheat the oven to 150°C (300°F). Grease and line a 30 × 23 × 4 cm (12 × 9 × 1½ in) baking tin with baking paper.

Put 300 g (10½ oz) of the liquorice in a small saucepan and add just enough water to cover, approximately 200 ml (7 fl oz). Place over a low heat and simmer for 15 minutes or until the liquorice has begun to break down. You want it to look like chunky black tar. Remove from the heat and allow to cool slightly before blitzing the whole soupy lot in a food processor to eradicate any remaining chunks of liquorice – we want a browny-black goop. Scrape into a bowl while it is still warm and set aside. Chop the remaining liquorice into small pieces and set aside.

In the bowl of an electric mixer fitted with the paddle attachment, beat the butter and both sugars until pale and creamy, about 5 minutes. Add the eggs one at a time, beating well after each addition. Scrape the liquorice mixture in and beat until incorporated. Turn the mixer to low and add the cocoa powder and a generous pinch of salt and continue to mix until combined. Turn off the mixer and, using a spatula, scrape down the sides of the bowl and give the mixture a few turns to get any bits at the bottom. Add the flour and stir to combine.

Pour the batter into the prepared tin and gently scatter over the chopped liquorice. Bake for 40–50 minutes. You want to see the slightest softness in the centre to ensure you have brownie, not cake – a good brownie needs a touch of sludgy fudgy in the middle and a top that looks like cracked earth. Scatter with sea salt flakes and allow to cool in the tin.

Store any leftover brownie in the fridge but remember my cardinal rule: a cold cake is not a good cake. The same applies to brownie. Let it come to a nice ambient room temp before inhaling.

24 carat

TRILLIONAIRE'S SHORTBREAD

With smoked almonds, pink peppercorns, violets and sea salt, enter stage left the world's most bougie caramel slice. Obvs with these toppings, this one is for you, not your local fundraising fete.

Gloriously smoky and salty, with a warming heat from pink peppercorns and the floral delight of crystallised violets, this is where it's at. You can also ditch the extras and make a very excellent slice if adornments and frippery aren't your thing. Turns out they are mine.

SHORTBREAD LAYER

165 g (6 oz) unsalted butter at room temperature, chopped

75 g (2¾ oz) caster (superfine) sugar

1 tablespoon vanilla bean paste

½ teaspoon salt

200 g (7 oz) plain (all-purpose) flour

CARAMEL LAYER

100 g (3½ oz) unsalted butter

100 g (3½ oz) rapadura sugar (or caster/superfine sugar)

395 g (14 oz) tin condensed milk

155 g (5½ oz/1 cup) smoked almonds, chopped, plus extra for topping

½–1 teaspoon salt flakes (or to taste)

TOP LAYER

220 g (8 oz/1¼ cups) milk chocolate chips, melted

crystallised violets, sea salt flakes and pink peppercorns

SERVES 12

Preheat the oven to 180°C (360°F). Line a 20 cm (8 in) round or square baking tin with baking paper.

For the shortbread layer, cream the butter and sugar in an electric mixer until pale and creamy. Add the vanilla bean paste and salt and mix briefly to incorporate. Add the flour and beat briefly to combine to a crumbly mixture. Press the mixture down across the base of the tin in an even layer. Bake in the oven until lightly golden, about 20 minutes.

For the caramel layer, put the butter, sugar and condensed milk in a saucepan over a medium heat. Stir vigorously to combine and simmer for up to 5 minutes, or until the mixture has thickened considerably and starts to come away from the sides. Stir through the chopped almonds and sea salt, then pour the caramel over the shortbread base and pop in the fridge for about 2 hours to set.

Once set, pour the melted milk chocolate over the caramel layer. Allow it to set lightly, about 1 minute, then scatter over the toppings at will. Refrigerate until ready to serve. Bring to room temperature before cutting with a hot, wet knife.

Extravagance in a tin
RASPBERRY MALT LOADED BROOKIES SLAB

When you are a complicated person, one who wants a brownie but also wants a cookie, this is the baked version of your indecision. A true hybrid of the two. There is malt, there is raspberry, there is chocolate. There is salt for balance and a satiation of need that goes beyond hunger. Also, if you do know what you want from life, i.e. a brownie or a cookie, both of these batters stand alone rather marvellously.

These brookies freeze like a dream for lunch boxes or late-night delights. If like me, you freeze chocolate goods to slow down how rapidly you eat them, it's also weirdly delicious frozen and chewy.

MALT CHOC COOKIE

125 g (4½ oz) unsalted butter

160 g (5½ oz) caster (superfine) sugar

3 tablespoons liquid malt

1 teaspoon vanilla bean paste

1 large egg

55 g (2 oz) Dutch (unsweetened) cocoa powder

50 g (1¾ oz) milk powder

125 g (4½ oz) plain (all-purpose) flour

½ teaspoon baking powder

pinch of sea salt flakes

150 g (5½ oz) couverture milk chocolate chips

BLONDIE

200 g (7 oz) unsalted butter

320 g (11½ oz) brown sugar

2 large free-range eggs

1 tablespoon vanilla bean paste

200 g (7 oz) plain (all-purpose) flour

150 g (5½ oz) couverture white chocolate chips

pinch of sea salt flakes

TO TOP

¾ cup frozen raspberries

milk and white chocolate chips

sea salt flakes

SERVES 12

Preheat the oven to 170°C (340°F). Grease and line a 30 × 23 × 5 cm (12 × 9 × 2 in) baking tin with baking paper.

For the malt choc cookie batter, put the butter, caster sugar and liquid malt in a saucepan over a low heat and stir constantly until the butter is melted and the sugar has dissolved. Remove from the heat and stir through the vanilla bean paste. Allow to cool slightly but, while still warm, add the egg and stir to fully incorporate. Whisk in the cocoa powder, milk powder, flour, baking powder and a generous pinch of sea salt flakes until fully combined. Throw in the milk chocolate chips, stir through briefly then pop in the fridge. Don't worry if it seems runny, it will firm up beautifully in the fridge.

To make the blondie batter, rinse out your saucepan or use another one and melt the butter until it is foaming and golden brown. Add the brown sugar and whisk vigorously. Allow to cool slightly then whisk in the eggs and vanilla bean paste to combine. Add the flour, white chocolate chips and a generous pinch of sea salt flakes and stir to combine.

Scoop blobs of blondie batter into the prepared tin. Ditto the cookie batter you had stored in the fridge. It should look like one of those old-school marble cakes with swirls of blondie and chocolate batter. Sprinkle over the frozen raspberries, milk and white chocolate chips and a generous smattering of sea salt flakes. Bake for 30 minutes. It should look golden and still have the slightest wobble in the centre. Allow to cool completely in the tin before serving.

Cut and come again

Simple PISTACHIO and ELDERFLOWER POUND CAKE

There is something special about a simple cake. One without all the heights of icing or filling, one that stands proud on the traditional simplicity of eggs, butter, sugar and flour.

I've gussied this up with some elderflower and pistachio, but this is my go-to pound cake base. You can add nothing more than vanilla or follow my path with a few bits and bobs. The possibilities are endless, and it's a great way to use up some fruit dregs or sweet spices on their last legs.

Florence White, writing in her 1932 collection of recipes, *Good Things in England*, references 'the cut-and-come-again-cakes that you never tire of'. This is absolutely one of those.

180 g (6½ oz) unsalted butter

250 g (9 oz) caster (superfine) sugar

3 large organic eggs

1 tablespoon vanilla bean extract

2 tablespoons elderflower cordial

grated zest of 1 large lemon

200 g (7 oz) plain (all-purpose) flour (or low-protein cake flour, if you have it)

1 heaped teaspoon baking powder

pinch of salt

125 ml (4 fl oz/½ cup) buttermilk

1–2 tablespoons pistachio paste

TOPPING

65 g (2 oz/½ cup) chopped pistachios

3 tablespoons raw (demerara) sugar

grated zest of 1 lemon

SERVES 8

Preheat the oven to 170°C (340°F). Grease and line a loaf (bar) tin with baking paper, leaving a little extra hanging over the precipice.

Beat the butter and sugar in the bowl of an electric mixer fitted with the paddle attachment until light and creamy. Add the eggs one at a time, beating thoroughly before adding the next. Add the vanilla bean extract, elderflower cordial and lemon zest. Add the flour, baking powder and a pinch of salt, beating briefly to incorporate, then add the buttermilk. Beat again briefly until well combined and you have a gloriously thick cake batter. Don't overwork it here.

Pour the batter into the loaf tin and drop on dollops of the pistachio paste. This will sink or stay – the mystery continues but is half the fun of eating this cake.

Bake for 20–25 minutes then turn the tin in your oven and cook for another 10 minutes – this helps ensure an evenly coloured crust. Check for doneness by inserting a skewer in the centre. It should come out mostly clean.

For the topping, quickly combine the chopped pistachios, sugar and lemon zest in a bowl. Open the oven door and scatter the mixture over the top of the cake, pushing down gently with your hand while being careful not to burn yourself. Cook for another 2–3 minutes. The mixture will adhere to the soft top of the batter, forming a glorious crust. You can add this afterwards instead, if you like, but note that it won't stick and you will have a little crumbly nut action all over your bench.

Let the cake cool completely in the tin before grabbing those paper edges and gently pulling the cake free for slicing.

The GOAT of muffins

FRUITS of the FOREST and WHITE CHOCOLATE MUFFINS

Muffins exist to legitimise eating cake for breakfast, free from the judgement of others. They are my food of choice come elevenses, and their portability makes them seem robust, even though the excellent ones are almost spilling inappropriately over the edges, teetering at capacity with the good stuff and delicate flower-like fragility.

In my mind, there is nothing quite like it come that afternoon dip, the sort that can only be dispelled with a bite of something sweet (this muffin) and tea. So these are unapologetically indulgent, moreish and should be on high rotation. They freeze like a dream and can be adapted so easily to suit whatever fruit is in season or your mood at the time.

125 g (4½ oz/1 cup) raspberries

250 g (9 oz) strawberries

100 g (3½ oz) rhubarb, trimmed and diced into small pieces (approx. 2 stalks)

handful mulberries (optional)

2 tablespoons brown sugar

225 g (8 oz/1½ cups) plain (all-purpose) flour

55 g (2 oz) almond meal

1 teaspoon baking powder

1 teaspoon bicarbonate of soda (baking soda)

140 g (5 oz) caster (superfine) sugar

grated zest of 1 lemon

pinch of salt

200 ml (7 fl oz) buttermilk

125 g (4½ oz) unsalted butter, melted

1 very generous teaspoon vanilla bean paste

1 large egg plus 1 yolk

150 g (5½ oz) caramelised white chocolate, chopped

CRUNCHY TOPPING

85 g (3 oz) plain (all-purpose) flour

2 tablespoons caster (superfine) sugar

2 tablespoons rolled (porridge) oats

pinch of sea salt flakes

50 g (1¾ oz) cold unsalted butter, cubed

icing (confectioners') sugar, for sprinkling (optional)

MAKES 8 JUMBO MUFFINS

Preheat the oven to 165°C (330°F). Grease and line a jumbo muffin tin. Set aside.

Put the fruit and brown sugar in a bowl and give them a gentle stir to combine. Set aside.

In a large bowl, combine the flour, almond meal, baking powder, bicarbonate of soda, caster sugar, lemon zest and a pinch of salt, stirring well to incorporate. Put the buttermilk, melted butter, vanilla bean paste, egg and yolk in a jug and whisk with a fork to combine, then pour over the dry ingredients, stirring gently to incorporate. Add the caramelised white chocolate and the fruit mixture, reserving a few tablespoons of fruit for the top of the muffins. Spoon the batter into the muffin cases until three-quarters full.

For the crunchy topping, combine the flour, sugar, oats and a pinch of sea salt flakes in a bowl. Toss through the butter, then use your fingertips to rub it into the dry ingredients until a finely clumped mixture has formed.

Top the muffins with the leftover fruit mixture and a very generous smattering of the crunchy topping.

Pop in the oven and cook for 30 minutes or until golden brown on top and cooked through.

SMACK

SNACKS

'Snacks' is a reductive term for such a spectacular and glorious way of eating. Why did we give the joy of the snack such loaded yet inconsequential terminology? There is so much to love about the meals enjoyed between other meals.

The French enjoy le goûter, while in Japan you have kuchisabishii, when you're not hungry but you eat because your mouth is 'lonely' – I mean, the beauty and acknowledgement of 'snacking' right there deserves some out-loud applause.

These are glorious snacks, the type that progress from snack to dinner with ease. Like any parent/responsible adult, I live in fear of those large afternoon teas that become an assault course of sugar combined with the bitter reality of a long, unstructured evening, because the idea of any kind of real dinner went tits-up at the third sticky bun. But these are the kind of snacks that are a natural segue to dinner. Savoury-focused, they can be built upon or even transformed into dinner themselves should the opportunity present itself.

The ultimate dip/dinner

REAL DEAL SOUR CREAM and ONION DIP with NON-NEGOTIABLE CHICKEN CRIMPIES

Time to curse the gods of expectation when it comes to food. Put that down like a plate straight from the oven, because everybody loves a good dip.

This slow-roasted French shallot dip (aka your ticket to decent French onion dip) is taking your humble Chicken Crimpie places. Good places. The jammy caramelised shallots with a tang of sour cream levitate this into the snacking stratosphere. Serve this with drinks and you'll be winning at life. And making friends.

12 French shallots, halved

3 tablespoons olive oil

3 tablespoons brown sugar

1 tablespoon chicken salt

pinch of sea salt flakes

4 tablespoons water

250 g (9 oz/1 cup) sour cream

125 g (4½ oz/½ cup) Kewpie mayonnaise

2 tablespoons buttermilk

grated zest of 1 lemon

1 garlic clove, grated

2–3 tablespoons finely chopped chives, plus more to scatter

Chicken Crimpies, to serve (if unavailable, substitute with a cracker of your choice)

MAKES ABOUT 2 CUPS

Preheat the oven to 160°C (320°F).

Put the French shallots, olive oil, brown sugar, chicken salt, 80 ml (2½ fl oz/⅓ cup) water and salt in a roasting tin. Give everything a good swoozsh then pop in the oven and cook until the shallots are caramelised and soft, between 45 minutes and 1 hour. Check on them from 40 minutes – you want them soft and yielding with a little bit of jammy juice on the tray.

Add three-quarters of the jammy shallots to a bowl along with the remaining ingredients. Gently fold through then place in a serving bowl. Top with the remaining shallots, scatter with the extra chives and season generously with salt and pepper.

Serve this epic bowl of goodness with Chicken Crimpies for the ultimate and most hedonistic snacking pleasure.

NOW, TO MAKE THIS DINNER … Throw some chicken thighs into a pan with some olive oil. Get some colour. Add the dip with a splash of chicken stock. Shove the pan in a 170°C (340°F) oven and roast until cooked through. Add salad. Dinner done. Life complete.

Nice buns ...

HARISSA HONEY BUTTER ROLLS

This is your foray into glory. I'll be honest, bread-making in all its forms is not my strength, despite my spectacular ability to eat it rapidly and often. But these puppies, they work every single time. They are respectable. They are slightly larger than a dinner roll but smaller than a burger bun so essentially made for snacking. I serve them at barbecues as much as I shove them in kids' lunchboxes or eat warm, just because, straight from the oven and slathered in even more butter and salt.

600 g (1 lb 5 oz/4 cups) strong flour
1 tablespoon sea salt flakes
375 ml (12½ fl oz/1½ cups) milk, plus an extra splash
90 g (3 oz/¼ cup) honey
50 g (1¾ oz) salted butter
4 teaspoons instant dried yeast
2 drops liquid smoke (optional)
2 eggs plus 1 egg yolk
olive oil for greasing

HONEY HARISSA BUTTER

½ tablespoon harissa paste (or more to taste)
3 tablespoons honey
125 g (4½ oz) unsalted butter

MAKES 12 ROLLS

Generously butter a 30 × 23 cm (12 × 9 in) baking tin and set aside.

Put the flour and salt in an electric mixer fitted with a dough hook and mix until combined.

Gently warm the milk, honey and butter in a saucepan. You want the butter to be melted but the mixture to remain a tepid temperature. Allow it to cool if it gets too hot before proceeding. Whisk in the yeast with a fork and set aside until foaming. Add the liquid smoke here if using.

Pour the wet mixture into the dry ingredients and combine briefly. Add the 2 eggs and beat on medium speed for 5–8 minutes – the dough will be tacky to the touch but should look smooth and come away from the bowl.

Scoop out the dough, using it to collect any leftover bits in the bowl. Grease the bowl with a little olive oil then return the dough and cover with a clean tea (dish) towel and allow to rise for 30 minutes in a warm spot (up to 45 minutes in cold weather).

After it has risen, divide the dough into 12 equal pieces about 80 g (2¾ oz) each (if you want to be pedantic about even-sized rolls). Roll them into balls, pinching the base of each so they look smooth and round.

Transfer the dough balls to the buttered tray, ensuring space around them to rise again. Set aside for 1 hour (or up to 2 hours in cold weather) until doubled in size and the balls are snug in the tin.

Preheat the oven to 175°C (345°F).

Lightly beat the egg yolk and splash of milk together and brush the rolls generously with the egg wash before popping in the oven for 18 minutes. They should look golden on top and bounce back when lightly pressed.

For the honey harissa butter, put the harissa, honey and butter in a small saucepan over a low heat. Stir until the butter has melted and the ingredients are incorporated. While the rolls are still hot, brush with the honey harissa butter and season generously with sea salt flakes.

Such a good egg

MASSAMAN CURRIED EGGS

Devilled eggs, that hot promise of the seventies, has been given the mildest of glow-ups. There is not much point messing with perfection, but the smoky, fragrant undertone of massaman is a brilliant bedfellow for the creamy egg.

Obvs you should add the paste slowly and gently, tasting as you go. Depending on which sort you get your hands on, massaman can vary in heat.

8 eggs

125 g (4½ fl oz/½ cup) Kewpie mayonnaise

3 teaspoons excellent-quality massaman curry paste, or to taste

TO SERVE

2–3 makrut lime leaves, stems removed, leaves finely sliced

Thai basil leaves

fried shallots

MAKES 16 AS A WEE SNACK

Gently lower the eggs into a saucepan of boiling water using a spoon, then cook until hard-boiled (10 minutes). Drain and refresh for 10 minutes in a bowl of iced water.

Peel the eggs and halve lengthways. Scoop out the yolks with a spoon and put them in a bowl with the mayonnaise and curry paste. Mash with a fork and season with salt and pepper to taste, adding more massaman if you like.

Spoon the yolk mixture into the halved whites. Scatter with the sliced makrut lime leaves, Thai basil leaves and shallots and serve immediately.

Any leftover eggs will last for up to 3 days in an airtight container in the fridge.

Made for the stage

TARTE FLAMBE

250 g (9 oz) flour, preferably strong white, plus extra for dusting

½ teaspoon salt, plus extra for seasoning

50 ml (1¾ fl oz) neutral oil

2 large onions

1 tablespoon unsalted butter

100 g (3½ oz) smoked streaky bacon or pancetta, preferably in one piece then cut into lardons

100 g (3½ oz) crème fraiche

60 g (2 oz/⅔ cup) finely grated parmesan

pinch of freshly grated nutmeg

SERVES 8

If I had the sort of career that required a subtly food-related stage name, 'Tarte Flambe' would be it. I also quite like Honey Popcorn but that's for another time. My point is, this is the kind of snack that needs a chaperone.

This Alsatian speciality took its stage show to Germany where it enjoys an equally spectacular name, Flammkuchen.

It is a thinner, crispier-based style of pizza. I've kept to the traditional pairings here, because in this case I do believe there is absolutely no reason to mess with perfection.

This is destined for a life well lived as snacks with drinks.

Start by making the base. Mix the flour and salt in a large bowl. In a jug, whisk 150 ml (5 fl oz) water and the oil, then gradually pour into the flour bowl and mix until you have a smooth dough. Continue mixing until it feels elastic, then cover and leave to rest for an hour.

Meanwhile, peel and finely slice the onion (if you have one, a mandoline would be helpful here).

Melt the butter in a frying pan over a medium heat and fry the bacon until the fat begins to render, then scoop it out with a slotted spoon and set aside, keeping as much fat in the pan as possible. Turn down the heat, add the onions and a pinch of salt and cook until soft and golden but not browned. Remove from the heat and allow to cool, then mix the crème fraiche and parmesan into the onions and season generously with the nutmeg.

Preheat the oven to 250°C (480°F) or as hot as it will go and place a lightly oiled baking tray inside to heat as well.

On a lightly floured surface, roll or stretch out the dough into a rectangle roughly the size of your tray and 1–2 mm thick. There is no need to get out a ruler so let common sense prevail – you just want a nice and thin stretched dough for maximum crispiness. Take the hot baking tray out of the oven and carefully transfer the dough base onto it, then spread the onion mixture over the surface.

Scatter the lardons all over the top, then bake for about 12 minutes until the edges are crisp and well browned (the timing will depend on how hot your oven gets, so keep a beady eye on it). Cut into squares and serve immediately.

Mouth carnival

CHEAT'S SPRING ONION and THAI BASIL PANCAKES with TIGER BITE SAUCE

I love me a spring onion pancake, but the hands-on labour involved when I just want a snack makes me feel the need to form a union and march the streets in protest for better working conditions.

This is a quick 'n' dirty version that is literally inhaled by adults and kids alike, so much so that there is always someone doing the roof-of-mouth burn dance when they can't wait for them to cool. It's usually me. Totally worth it.

1 cup finely sliced spring onions (scallions)

1 cup finely chopped Thai basil leaves

275 g (9½ oz) dumpling wrappers (round white wrappers work best) at room temperature

neutral oil for brushing pancakes and frying

TIGER BITE SAUCE

1 heaped cup sweet cherry tomatoes

1 tablespoon caster (superfine) sugar

2 garlic cloves, chopped

2 tablespoons sweet soy sauce

1 tablespoon oyster sauce

1 teaspoon fish sauce

juice of 1 lime

1 red chilli, seeds removed and finely diced (to taste, or leave out altogether for kids)

SERVES 8

Put the spring onions and Thai basil in a bowl and gently toss to combine. Set aside.

For the tiger bite sauce, put all the ingredients plus ⅓ cup of the combined spring onions and Thai basil in a blender and blitz until it has a chunky salsa-like consistency. Pour into a bowl and set aside.

To make the pancakes, brush a dumpling wrapper with oil. Add about 1 teaspoon of the spring onion and Thai basil mixture, season with a few sea salt flakes and press another wrapper on top, like you were making a sandwich. Repeat this layering process until you have used about five wrappers. Don't oil the top of the last wrapper – you want to avoid it sticking to your rolling pin. Use a rolling pin to gently roll the pancake out until it is approximately one and a half times its original size. You can experiment here – minimal rolling makes for a thicker pancake, more rolling will mean a thinner, crispier pancake. Repeat with the remaining wrappers and herb mix.

(At this point you can layer your rolled pancakes between sheets of baking paper and freeze for another time – great if you have leftover wrappers and chopped herbs.)

Add a decent lug of oil to a frying pan and place over a medium heat. Once hot and shimmering, add the pancakes one at a time and cook for up to a minute each side or until they look golden and crisp. Some spots will be crisp, some will be chewy – this is all part of the excellence.

Season generously with sea salt flakes and serve with the tiger bite sauce.

Kid-approved
CHEDDARMITE DELIGHT

2 teaspoons instant dried yeast

2 teaspoons honey

2 tablespoons olive oil, plus extra for greasing

375 ml (12½ fl oz/1½ cups) tepid water

600 g (1 lb 5 oz/4 cups) strong flour, plus extra for dusting

2 teaspoons sea salt flakes

3 tablespoons milk powder

Vegemite to taste

350 g (12½ oz/4 loosely packed cups) grated cheddar cheese

EGG WASH

1 egg yolk

1 tablespoon milk

SERVES 10

The only thing wrong with those sneaky bakery-chain cheddarmite scrolls, aside from the walk of shame carrying the sweating plastic bag of the goods down the street, is they are over before they've even begun.

This loaf is the love child of a cheddarmite scroll and a hack's shokupan (Japanese milk bread) using milk powder rather than milk.

I need cheap thrills, so I rammed the lot into a straight-sided Pullman tin because I love that glorious top puffing out like a carbohydrate peacock.

Best eaten on the day of making.

Combine the yeast, honey, olive oil and water in a jug. Set aside until you see little spores fluffing across the surface like a science experiment.

In the bowl of an electric mixer fitted with a dough hook, mix the flour, salt and milk powder on low to combine. Add the yeast mixture and knead on medium for 5–8 minutes or until the dough looks smooth and has completely come away from the sides of the bowl. Cover the bowl with a clean tea (dish) towel and leave it to prove at room temperature for an hour or until it has at least doubled in size.

Preheat the oven to 200°C (390°F). Generously grease a Pullman or loaf (bar) tin and set aside.

Lightly flour your kitchen bench. Turn out the dough and roll it out until you have about a 1 cm (½ in) thickness. Spread over some Vegemite as liberally or as lightly as you like it with about a 1 cm (½ in) border along all sides. Where there is Vegemite, cover in cheese.

Now roll it up. I do not follow a prescribed method for this: the simplest thing to do is roll and fold in the edges like you are making a wrap for lunch. However you do it, the key is to pinch down firmly where the dough joins together on the rolled edge – you want to create a sealed seam to prevent any of the cheesy filling from escaping. Place it into the tin seam side down so you have a nice smooth top.

Allow to rest in the tin for 30 minutes at room temperature.

Make the egg wash by whisking the egg yolk and milk in a small bowl with a fork. Brush over the top of the loaf, which should now be popping over the top of the tin after the second rise.

Pop in the oven and cook for 25–30 minutes. Allow to cool in the pan before removing and cutting into indecently thick slices with a bread knife.

For the love of cheese

BAKED FETA with SIZZLING THYME, SUMAC, HONEY and HERBS

This is not the baked feta making its way around that thing called TikTok. This is just a perfect snackfest that felt imperative to include. It's a dump and bake situation with high reward. And the best bit is seeing the realisation in others that caramelised honey is a pot of gold – you want to scrape at it in the dish while it's still warm and stretchy. It'd be rude not to – at the very least it helps with the washing up.

200 g (7 oz) block of Greek-style feta

3 tablespoons olive oil

2 tablespoons honey

1 teaspoon dried thyme

THE CRUNCHER

60 g (2 oz) pistachios, toasted and chopped

2 teaspoons sumac

grated zest of 1 lemon

2–3 tablespoons fresh thyme leaves

½ tablespoon sea salt flakes

SERVES 6

Preheat the oven to 180°C (360°F).

Put the feta in a small ovenproof dish. Drizzle over the olive oil, honey and dried thyme. Pop in the oven for 20 minutes.

While the feta is baking, combine all the cruncher ingredients in a bowl.

Remove the feta and, while still hot, sprinkle over the cruncher very liberally. Serve while nice and warm with bread or crackers or whatever else you might find in your cupboard that is carbohydrate-informed enough to work.

ROASTED LEEK and AJVAR GOZLEME of SORTS

Like some kind of ancient reflex, your hand just reaches for them. Again and again.

This recipe calls for mild ajvar, a spread that is popular across south-eastern Europe and includes roasted capsicums, tomatoes and sometimes chilli.

I have taken a similar path to a gozleme here, but mine is closer to a pizza pocket vibe in order to minimise dough rolling and folding, making these a speedier snack option.

350 g (12½ oz) plain (all-purpose) flour, plus extra for dusting

½ tablespoon fine sea salt flakes

1 teaspoon baking powder

60 ml (2 fl oz/¼ cup) olive oil, plus extra for frying

1 tablespoon Greek yoghurt

lemon wedges, to serve

FILLING

2 leeks, white part only, sliced lengthways

olive oil for drizzling

120 g (4½ oz/½ cup) Persian feta

85 g (3 oz/⅓ cup) mild ajvar

SERVES 6

Preheat the oven to 170°C (340°F).

Start the filling by popping the leek halves on a roasting tin lined with baking paper and drizzling over a generous lug of olive oil. Give them a gentle toss with your hands to coat then roast in the oven for 30–45 minutes or until golden and soft. You will need to check on them as the cooking time will vary depending on size. Once cooked through, roughly chop the roasted flesh. When cooled, combine with the feta in a bowl and set aside.

For the dough, combine the flour, salt and baking powder in a large bowl. Add the olive oil, yoghurt and 100 ml (3½ fl oz) water. Stir until everything is well combined. If it seems dry and crumbly, add more water a tablespoon at a time until you get a nice dough consistency.

Flour your work surface, turn out the dough and knead it for about 3 minutes until smooth and elastic. Cover with plastic wrap or a clean tea (dish) towel and set aside for 15 minutes to rest.

Divide the dough into three equal portions. Roll each piece into a rectangle about 25 × 15 cm (10 × 6 in). This is a rough guide – don't go getting out a ruler. I like to keep the dough thicker than a traditional gozleme to ensure the filling doesn't escape. It also helps to stop it tearing and avoids all that rolling labour on your part.

Have the shorter edge of dough nearest you and spread the bottom half with a third of the ajvar, leaving a 1 cm (½ in) border around all the edges to help with folding. Top the ajvar with about a third of the leek and feta mixture. It's important not to get overexcited with the filling here – if you overfill, the pastry will tear and you'll get a bit of an oozy mess. Not the end of the world, because ooze is delicious, but it just helps for containment when frying. Fold down the top half of the dough to cover the fillings then fold the edges over and pinch together to seal. Repeat with the other two pieces of dough and the remaining fillings.

Gently lift each gozleme and dust generously with some flour on both sides. Place them pinched seam side up on your workbench and roll very gently to flatten out over the folded seam. Do this lightly so the filling doesn't explode out – it just helps to ensure a good seal. Don't be too fussed about shape as it will get cut up into slices anyway.

Whack a frying pan onto the hob over a medium heat. Add a lug of olive oil and, once hot, fry the gozleme one at a time until golden and crisp, about 3 minutes each side. Cut the gozleme into wedges, season with sea salt flakes and serve with lemon wedges. Eat piping hot at their delicious best.

Note: you can make the dough ahead of time and roll it out into sheets, separated by baking paper, then store covered in the fridge for up to 3 days.

A FEW Easy DESS- ERTS

Dessert can and should traverse the distance between 'just a sweet something' to 'a bowl of decadence' with ease. And you can achieve both without any great complexity, cooking time or labour.

All of these can be made ahead, with a few simple final flourishes that can easily be done post-dinner and a few drinks deep.

When life gives you lemons
PRESERVED- LEMON kind of BOMBE ALASKA

Don't mean to toot my own horn but toot. This is bloody genius. Thank goodness for preserved lemons now finding their way into aisle-seven territory of most supermarkets. Combined here with a tub of ice cream, the lemons do the magic thing of tempering the sweetness while adding a deeper, funkier tang without the cat's bum mouth hit of acidity. It tastes a bit 'restauranty' in that it is unexpected yet completely delicious. Add the burnt meringue for a touch of fance and this is the dessert dreams are made of.

1 litre (34 fl oz/4 cups) decent-quality vanilla ice cream

¼–1 preserved lemon, rinsed and seeds removed, chopped

6 large lemons, halved lengthways, flesh removed and reserved for another use

lemon zest or edible flowers, to serve (optional)

MERINGUE

2 egg whites

110 g (4 oz) caster (superfine) sugar

¼ teaspoon cornflour (cornstarch)

¼ teaspoon white vinegar

MAKES 12

Blitz the ice cream and preserved lemon in a blender until combined. Work quickly here – you want a McDonald's shake consistency, not a runny liquid. If you are unsure about the strength of the preserved lemon, just add it in gradually and taste as you go until you get sweet mixed with a gloriously deep, muted tang.

Spoon the ice cream into your lemon halves level with the cut peel, then cover and pop in the freezer for at least 3 hours to set. Wedging them snugly together in a dish lined with baking paper avoids any toppling over during the freeze.

When ready to serve, prepare the meringue by whisking the egg whites in an electric mixer on high speed until stiff peaks form (1–2 minutes). Gradually add the sugar, whisking continuously, until stiff and shiny (up to 4 minutes), then add the cornflour and vinegar and whisk again to combine.

Spoon some meringue on the top of each set lemon, using your spoon to shape it or just plopping it and moving on. Toast the meringue all over with a kitchen blowtorch set on medium until golden.

Scatter with lemon zest or edible flowers, if using, and serve immediately.

CAN'T BE FAFFED If you can't be faffed with the meringue component, spoon in the ice cream, shove them in the freezer and serve as they are – they still taste great.

GIVE ME EXTRA Serve with a scattering of edible flowers or jasmine from the garden. The jasmine scent is amazing, and trust me – with the hit of lemon, it gives all the extra summer I-made-an-effort-for-you vibes without any of the actual effort. Winning.

A FEW EASY DESSERTS

Willy Wonka would be proud

VIOLET CRUMBLE for ADULTS

Violet Crumbles are in the happy business. No one eats chocolate-coated honeycomb and remains unhappy – it's impossible.

This crunch is childhood delight personified. You get chocolate melting between your fingers with the odd bit of the 'comb illicitly wedged between your teeth to enjoy for hours afterwards.

420 g (15 oz/1¾ cups) caster (superfine) sugar

155 g (5½ oz) glucose syrup

70 g (2½ oz) honey

20 g (¾ oz) bicarbonate of soda (baking soda)

TO COAT

1 cup each white, milk and dark couverture chocolate chips

crystallised violets, freeze-dried fruit or whatever your heart desires to scatter

MAKES ABOUT 4 CUPS

Line a deep 20 cm (8 in) square baking tin with baking paper.

Put the caster sugar, glucose syrup, honey and 70 ml (2¼ fl oz) water in a medium saucepan over a medium–low heat. Stir to dissolve the sugar then bring to the boil. Cook until the mixture reaches 160°C (320°F) on a sugar thermometer, then remove from the heat and carefully add the bicarbonate of soda, whisking quickly to dissolve as it puffs and rages with dramatic flair. Pour into the prepared baking tin and set aside to cool for at least 1 hour.

Once cool, break the honeycomb into large chunks and set aside in an airtight container.

To melt the chocolate, first bring a small saucepan half-filled with water to a boil, then turn off the heat and place a bowl over the top with the white chocolate chips in it until melted, stirring to incorporate. Repeat with remaining chocolate in separate bowls.

Line a large baking tray with baking paper. Dip about a third of the honeycomb chunks in the chocolate, turning gently with a spoon or your fingers to coat evenly. Shake lightly before transferring to the baking tray. Repeat with the milk and dark chocolate and the remaining pieces of honeycomb. Scatter over any extra decorations such as crystallised violets. Pop in the fridge to set for at least an hour then serve.

Will keep for a few weeks in an airtight container in the fridge.

For strawb lovers

SLOW-ROASTED STRAWBERRIES and CREAM with MILK CHOCOLATE CRUNCH

Roasting strawberries for three hours takes it past mush to something incredible and intense. Yes, you have to forward plan this one a little, but the oven is doing the work – you just have to shove them in and forget.

This is ideal for strawberry gluts at the peak of the season when they are going cheap.

This is an all-occasion, eat-anytime dessert, and I am here for it until the end of my days. It also makes more chocolate crunch than you need. Stow away for those days.

1 kg (2 lb 3 oz) strawberries, hulled

180 g (6½ oz/¾ cup) caster (superfine) sugar

2 tablespoons vanilla bean paste

360 g (12½ oz/1⅔ cups) mascarpone

CHOCOLATE CRUNCH

500 g (1 lb 2 oz) excellent-quality milk or dark chocolate chips

1¾ cups feuilletine flakes

SERVES 6

Preheat the oven to 150°C (300°F).

Spread the strawberries over a roasting tin and add the caster sugar and vanilla bean paste. Toss gently to coat, then pop in the oven and cook for 3 hours. The strawberries should be only just holding their shape and be a rich and beautiful dark red.

While the strawberries are roasting, prepare the chocolate crunch by putting the chocolate in a bowl that will fit snugly over a small saucepan half-filled with water, ensuring no water touches the bowl. Bring the water to a boil, then turn off the heat and let the chocolate sit and melt in peace. Give it a good stir until smooth then mix through the feuilletine flakes.

Line a baking tray with baking paper. Scoop the chocolate feuilletine mixture onto the tray and, using a palette knife, smooth the top surface. You can make this as thin or as thick as you like. Pop in the fridge to set.

When ready to serve, break the chocolate crunch into shards.

To serve, spoon ¼ cup of mascarpone into each serving glass or small bowl. Top with generous spoonfuls of roasted strawberries and add a few shards of chocolate crunch.

HOT TIP I buy the feuilletine (a crunchy wafer made from sweet crepes) online or from cake supply stores for the chocolate crunch. If you can't be bothered with that, crisp wafers or supermarket waffle cones that have been given a quick whizz in the blender make a worthy substitute.

A FEW EASY DESSERTS

The show-stopper

BLOOD PLUM PANNACOTTA for a CROWD with ORANGE BLOSSOM and BLACK PEPPER

I get it: this dessert flavour combination sounds like some kind of gustatory trust fall performed on a retreat, but I promise it's worth the free dive. I strongly support the use of herbaceous elements in sweets – it pronounces their flavour while providing elements of cut-through from the sweetness. Here the pepper makes the orange blossom and sweetly tart plum juice bring out the very best in each other, while its sharpness puts all the creaminess of the pannacotta in its place.

600 ml (20½ fl oz) thickened (whipping) cream

225 g (8 oz/1½ cups) chopped couverture white chocolate

2½ titanium-strength gelatine leaves, bloomed in cold water

1.4 kg (3 lb 1 oz) vanilla bean yoghurt

1 tablespoon vanilla bean paste

3 tablespoons unsalted butter

60 g (2 oz/½ cup) slivered almonds

PLUM POUR-OVER

2 blood plums, sliced and seeds discarded (I love to use Queen Garnet plums)

1 tablespoon orange-blossom water

2 tablespoons caster (superfine) sugar

freshly cracked black pepper, to taste

TO TOP

2 blood plums, sliced and seeds discarded

125 g (4½ oz/1 cup) raspberries, halved

125 g (4½ oz) mulberries or blackberries

SERVES 8–12

To make the pannacotta, put the cream and chocolate in a saucepan over a low heat, stirring regularly until incorporated. Add the bloomed gelatine and whisk vigorously to combine. Remove from the heat and whisk through the yoghurt and vanilla bean paste. Pour into a large serving bowl (approximately 30 cm/12 in wide and at least 10 cm/4 in high) or large trifle bowl and place in the fridge to set. It's best to let this sit overnight or a minimum of 8 hours.

Put the butter in a small frying pan over a medium heat. Once foaming, add the slivered almonds and cook, stirring constantly, until golden and toasted. Remove with a slotted spoon to a plate lined with paper towel and set aside.

To make the plum pour-over, put the sliced plums, orange-blossom water and caster sugar in a saucepan over a low heat. Cook for 1–2 minutes or until the sugar has dissolved and the plums are starting to break down. Strain into a jug and season with a good crack of black pepper – it seems odd, but it makes the flavours come alive. Allow to cool.

To serve, spoon some of the plum pour-over onto the pannacotta, top with the extra sliced plums and berries, the toasted almonds and another light cracking of pepper.

HOT TIP I hate ruining stone fruit with stubborn seed removal, so I tend to slice my fruit as close to the stone as possible then discard the seed. If you have more luck than me, remove the stone first and then slice as per the recipe.

You will need to start this one day ahead.

Eating clouds and happiness

TURKISH DELIGHT PAV

In each of my books, meringue exists in some form as a nod to my grandmother. She taught me to cook long before I had any inkling of the hold it would have over my life, and the very smell of whisked egg whites and sugar is enough to take me out at the knees. I never had the opportunity to thank her, an eternal regret, but I can honour her in every book and every meringue.

I adore the wild entanglements of Turkish delight running through the peaks and troughs of this meringue like capillaries. It gives it both whimsy and a sense of occasion.

TURKISH DELIGHT SYRUP (MAKES ABOUT ¾ CUP)

170 g (6 oz) Turkish delight

250 ml (8½ fl oz/1 cup) water

PAVLOVA

8 egg whites at room temperature

450 g (1 lb) caster (superfine) sugar

1 tablespoon white-wine vinegar

1 tablespoon vanilla bean paste

TO TOP

150 g (5½ oz) thickened (whipping) cream

125 g (4½ oz/1 cup) raspberries

250 g (9 oz) strawberries, hulled and sliced

edible fresh rose petals (optional)

SERVES 8–10

To make the Turkish delight syrup, dust off as much of the sugar coating as possible from the Turkish delight pieces and chop into chunks if large. Put in a saucepan with 250 ml (8½ fl oz/1 cup) water and simmer on a very low heat, stirring regularly, until the Turkish delight dissolves and you are left with a gloriously gloopy syrup, similar in consistency to thick honey. This can take anywhere between 5 and 15 minutes. Allow to cool slightly.

Preheat the oven to 115°C (240°F). Line a large baking tray approximately 40 × 30 cm (15¾ × 12 in) with baking paper.

For the pavlova, whisk the egg whites and a small pinch of salt in the bowl of an electric mixer fitted with the whisk attachment until soft peaks form, about 4 minutes. Keep whisking while gradually adding the sugar until firm and glossy, another 3 minutes. Rub some of the mixture between two fingers – if it still feels grainy, continue whisking. Once smooth, whisk in the vinegar and vanilla bean paste.

Using a spoon, drizzle over a few spoonfuls of the Turkish delight syrup and then gently fold it through the meringue – you just want a few random streaks of pink. Scoop the meringue out onto your lined tray and drizzle over another tablespoon of the syrup. Use a palette knife or spatula to loosely swirl it over the top of the meringue – we only want ribbons of pink here and there through the meringue. Reserve the remaining syrup to serve.

Place the meringue in the oven and bake until crisp but not coloured, about 1½ hours. Turn off the heat and allow to cool completely in the oven. DO NOT SKIP THIS STEP.

To plate, gently transfer your meringue to a serving platter. Lightly whip the cream to medium–firm peaks and scoop it over the top of the meringue. Top with the berries, then drizzle over a little more Turkish delight syrup. Scatter with edible rose petals, if using, and serve.

The spice of life
MASALA BURNT BASQUE

1 kg (2 lb 3 oz) cream cheese

520 g (1 lb 2 oz) caster (superfine) sugar

250 g (9 oz) mascarpone

100 ml (3½ fl oz) pouring (single) cream

5 eggs plus 3 egg yolks

3 teaspoons each ground cardamom, ground cloves and ground cinnamon

1 tablespoon vanilla bean paste

SERVES 8–10

Think about all the very best cheese experiences in your life. These moments, more often than not, went with 'something', am I right? Cheese and quince, fondue with all its dippy, bready, appley goods ... In this case, it's masala. Ah, the smoky sweet delight of this fragrant goodness just gets in there like a nosy neighbour. To the core. It's so good, and it puts this dessert in another dimension.

PS: This is probably the easiest recipe in this book. It's a dump and run situation that brings applause and is hands down the easiest way to make a pretty bloody spectacular dessert for a crowd.

PPS: If you wanted to make it all traditional and conservative, just leave the spice combo out. It's still get-in-your-face delicious.

PPPS: You can add all of this to a blender, give her a swoozsh until all combined and pour in the tin. Voila. Not much more hands-off than that.

It is best to start this recipe a day before.

Preheat the oven to 200°C (390°F). Grease and line a round 25 cm (10 in) springform cake tin. Line it generously with baking paper so that it extends above the rim with a lot of drama-fuelled overhang.

Put all the ingredients in the bowl of an electric mixer fitted with the paddle attachment and beat on low until incorporated. You can also do this in a blender, but make sure it has a large capacity to fit everything in, with a big engine to boot!

Pop her in the oven and cook that puppy for 45 minutes until it looks like she fell asleep on a beach in Tijuana under the strength of a midday sun. She's tanned, but she's still going to have a roll to her. Stay calm and shove her in the fridge for a sleepover. We want a cheesecake meets crème brûlée centre kind of consistency.

Before serving, pull her from the fridge and give her some time at room temperature – a super cold cheesecake is a bad cheesecake. Slice and serve to adoration.

Total mouth party

Two-minute SOFT SERVE

3 cups frozen fruit

50 ml (1¾ fl oz) condensed milk

SOME FLAVOURS TO TRY

3 cups frozen pineapple

¼ cup mint leaves

50 ml (1¾ fl oz) condensed milk

3 cups frozen raspberries

50 ml (1¾ fl oz) condensed milk

1 cup dark chocolate chunks

3 cups frozen mango

squeeze of lime juice

3 makrut lime leaves, veins removed and very finely sliced

50 ml (1¾ fl oz) condensed milk

SERVES 6

Easiest dessert in all the lands. It's chuck-and-blend glory with a few basic ingredients, because there is nothing wrong with basic. This is uncomplicated and comforting and will become the dessert you serve on the hour on the daily, again and again, throughout summer.

You can add a little juju with herbs and the like, but there is nothing wrong with the one-two punch. See? Basic.

And as far as desserts go, it's really a very low condensed milk to fruit ratio, so it's whipped fruit more than anything else and is a real mouth pleaser for young and old.

Add the fruit, condensed milk and any additional flavours to a blender and blitz until you achieve a soft serve–like consistency. If using larger ingredients like chocolate chunks, stir these through at the end once you have blended the fruit with the condensed milk.

Serve immediately. This is best eaten on the day of making. If you've frozen leftovers, get it out to sit at room temperature for a few minutes before scooping into cups or cones to serve.

HOT TIP A squeeze of lemon or lime juice helps cut through the sweetness and makes the soft serve come alive.

INDEX

A PAGE
of THANKS

Books start with one but are executed by many. It took 20 months, 276 recipes, uncountable late nights, 16 burns and 3 knife nicks to get this book into your hands. And a tribe. A tribe of people who (luckily for me) have an infallible belief in this book.

Simon Davis. For steering the ship the best way possible and for being unflappable in the face of a cook who wants to measure the heat of a curry by the level of tit sweat. (Maybe the next book?). Thank you – the process has been such a joy.

Antonietta Anello. Thank you for keeping the motivation going, keeping the schedule on track, the queries flowing and for being a cookbook whisperer and pushing this book into new and better territory.

Simone Ford. A recipe is only as good as the eye that edits it. Thank you for keeping my voice but making sure I measure everything to the ml rather than a splosh of this and a lug of that. This is the shiniest, most accurate it can be because of you. Thank you for doing the words and the lines that I can't bear to do.

Erica Brown. What a playground find! My creative soul sister and phantom limb when it comes to execution. Can't and won't do a book without you and that astute eye of yours. Thank you.

Emily O'Neill. For bringing the colour and the energy and the fun. I'm allergic to pomp and circumstance. Thank you for understanding this and keeping this bright, relaxed and the opposite of sterile. Cookbooks, like the cooks that hold them, should be fun and generous.

To the publishers a lifetime ago who said no – a word I don't like but I find incredibly motivating. Weirdly, thanks for making me a dog at a bone for a yes.

And to my Hardie Grant crew – sometimes you find a publisher that fits like a glove. So lucky to be in the house. Roxy, marketing, the sales team on the ground. Thank you for always believing in me and pushing this into the universe.

And lastly and most importantly. Tom. Lulu. Claude. Eddie. My books leech into our everyday life and you accept and embrace them. Thank you for being my harshest recipe critics and greatest champions. Every page is for you.

ABOUT *the* AUTHOR

Katrina Meynink is an author, food stylist, and culinary creative known for her vibrant, flavoursome and approachable recipes that leave nothing on the cutting board. *Kitchen Keepers: Real-Life Recipes to Make on Repeat* is her sixth book; one she has written in between her columns for popular Australian website *Good Food* and negotiating dinnertime peace deals between her three kids and their dog.

With a passion for excellent ingredients and a love for home cooking, Katrina has made a name for herself in the culinary world, blending flavour combinations and techniques she has garnered through her education and years of experience as a recipe developer. Her approach balances her hedonistic intent with weeknight convenience.

When she's not crafting delicious recipes, you can find her attempting to grow herbs in her garden — usually with more enthusiasm than success, or testing something delicious in her woodfired oven to share with family and friends.

BUT WAIT — what's a cookbook without a roast chook?

Slow-roasted CHICKEN in CHORIZO SAUCE

Roast chook, an unimpeachable classic. Abhorrent that I almost didn't put one in. A roast chicken is the food that feeds. It feeds the belly, it feeds the soul and it feeds conversation.

There will be leftover chorizo sauce with this, so freeze it. Make this chicken again using the sauce, or use it as a pasta sauce of dreams.

60 g (2 oz) salted butter, softened

1½ tablespoons tomato paste (concentrated purée)

2 garlic cloves, crushed

1 tablespoon finely chopped oregano leaves

1 chicken, butterflied

a few strands of cherry tomatoes on the vine

25 g (1 oz/¼ cup) freshly grated parmesan, to serve

sea salt flakes and freshly ground black pepper, to season

CHORIZO SAUCE

2 tablespoons olive oil, plus extra for drizzling

2 fresh chorizo sausages, casings removed and meat finely chopped

1 large onion, finely diced

4 garlic cloves, crushed

3 tablespoons oregano leaves

1 tablespoon dried oregano

500 ml (17 fl oz/2 cups) white wine

500 ml (17 fl oz/2 cups) tomato passata (puréed tomatoes)

1 tablespoon brown sugar

SERVES 5

To make the chorizo sauce, heat the olive oil in a large frying pan over a medium–low heat. Once hot, fry the chorizo meat and onion until the onion has softened and the chorizo has released its lovely orange oils into the pan. Add the garlic and fresh and dried oregano and cook for another minute or so until fragrant. Stir in the wine, passata and sugar and let it simmer while you prepare the chicken. You want to give the sauce 20 minutes to reduce and to ensure the flavours become well-acquainted.

Preheat the oven to 180°C (360°F).

Combine the butter, tomato paste, garlic and oregano in a bowl. Lay the chicken, skin side up, on a flat work surface. Working gently, lift the skin of the chicken and spread the butter mixture across the breasts, pushing it into as many crevices as possible without tearing the skin. Season the chicken generously with sea salt flakes and freshly ground black pepper.

Carefully pour the chorizo sauce into a roasting tin. Plonk the chicken on top and drizzle over a little olive oil. Add the tomatoes on the vine and pop in the oven for 1 hour and 20 minutes. If the skin of the chicken looks like it needs a tan after that, you can turn the oven to the grill (broiler) function for a minute or two for the ultimate crispy golden skin.

Just before serving, scatter over the parmesan and season with sea salt flakes and freshly ground black pepper.

Published in 2025 by Hardie Grant Books, an imprint of Hardie Grant Publishing

Hardie Grant Books (Melbourne)
Wurundjeri Country
Level 11, 36 Wellington Street
Collingwood, Victoria 3066

Hardie Grant North America
2912 Telegraph Ave
Berkeley, California 94705

hardiegrant.com/books

Hardie Grant acknowledges the Traditional Owners of the Country on which we work, the Wurundjeri People of the Kulin Nation and the Gadigal People of the Eora Nation, and recognises their continuing connection to the land, waters and culture. We pay our respects to their Elders past and present.

 A catalogue record for this book is available from the National Library of Australia

Kitchen Keepers: Real-life Recipes to Make on Repeat
ISBN 978 1 76145 065 5

10 9 8 7 6 5 4 3 2 1

Publisher: Simon Davis
Head of Editorial: Jasmin Chua
Project Editor: Antonietta Anello
Editor: Simone Ford
Creative Director: Kristin Thomas
Designer and Illustrator: Emily O'Neill
Head of Production: Todd Rechner
Production Controller: Jessica Harvie

Colour reproduction by Splitting Image Colour Studio
Printed in China by Leo Paper Products LTD.

The paper this book is printed on is from FSC®-certified forests and other sources. FSC® promotes environmentally responsible, socially beneficial and economically viable management of the world's forests.